Welcome to
Table Talk

Table Talk helps children and adults explore the Bible together. Each day provides a short family Bible time which, with your own adaptation, could work for ages 4 to 12. It includes optional follow on material which takes the passage further for older children. There are also suggestions for linking **Table Talk** with **XTB** children's notes.

> **Who can use Table Talk?**

- **Families**
- **One adult with one child**
- **A teenager with a younger brother or sister**
- **Children's leaders with their groups**
- **Any other mix that works for you!**

TableTalk

A short family Bible time for daily use. Table Talk takes about five minutes, maybe at breakfast, or after an evening meal. Choose whatever time and place suits you best as a family. Table Talk includes a simple discussion starter or activity that leads into a short Bible reading. This is followed by a few questions.

XTB

XTB children's notes help 7-11 year olds to get into the Bible for themselves. They are based on the same Bible passages as **Table Talk**. You will find suggestions for how **XTB** can be used alongside **Table Talk** on the next page.

In the next three pages you'll find suggestions for how to use Table Talk, along with hints and tips for adapting it to your own situation. If you've never done anything like this before, check out our Table Talk web page for further help (see website addresses below) or write in for a fact sheet.

THE SMALL PRINT

Table Talk is published by The Good Book Company, 37 Elm Road, New Malden, Surrey, KT3 3HB, UK.
Written by Alison Mitchell (alison@thegoodbook.co.uk) and Mark Tomlinson. Fab pictures by Kirsty McAllister.
Printed in China. Bible quotations taken from the Good News Bible. **UK:** www.thegoodbook.co.uk
N America: www.thegoodbook.com **Australia:** www.thegoodbook.com.au **New Zealand:** www.thegoodbook.co.nz

HOW TO USE
Table Talk

Table Talk is designed to last for up to three month[s]. How you use it depends on what works for you. W[e] have included 65 full days of material in this issue plus some more low-key suggestions for another 2[5] days (at the back of the book). We would like to encourage you to work establishing a pattern of family reading. The first two weeks are the harde[st].

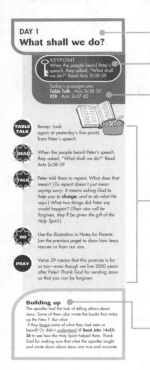

DAY 1
What shall we do?

KEYPOINT
When the people heard Peter's speech, they asked, "What shall we do?" Read Acts 2v38-39

Today's passages are:
Table Talk Acts 2v38-39
XTB Acts 2v37-40

TABLE TALK — Recap: Look again at yesterday's five points from Peter's speech.

READ — When the people heard Peter's speech, they asked, "What shall we do?" Read Acts 2v38-39

TALK — Peter told them to repent. What does that mean? (*To repent doesn't just mean saying sorry. It means asking God to help you to change, and to do what He says.*) What two things did Peter say would happen? (*Their sins will be forgiven, they'll be given the gift of the Holy Spirit.*)

DO — Use the illustration in Notes for Parents (*on the previous page*) to show how Jesus rescues us from our sins.

PRAY — Verse 39 means that this promise is for us too—even though we live 2000 years after Peter! Thank God for sending Jesus so that you can be forgiven.

Building up
The apostles had the task of telling others about Jesus. Some of them also wrote the books that make up the New T. But what if they forgot some of what they had seen or heard? Or didn't understand it? **Read John 14v25-26** to see how the Holy Spirit helped them. Thank God for making sure that what the apostles taught and wrote down about Jesus was true and accurate.

Table Talk is based on the same Bible passages as *XTB*, but usually only asks for two or three verses to be read out loud. The full *XTB* passage is listed at the top of each **Table Talk** page. If you are using **Table Talk** with older children, read the full *XTB* passage rather than the shorter version.

KEYPOINT
This is the main point you should be trying to convey. Don't read this out—it often gives away the end of the story!

The main part of **Table Talk** is designed to be suitable for younger children. **Building Up** includes more difficult questions designed for older children, or those with more Bible knowledge.

As far as possible, if your children are old enough to read the Bible verses for themselves, encourage them to find the answers in the passage and to tell you which verse the answer is in. This will help them to get used to handling the Bible for themselves.

The **Building Up** section is designed to build on the passage studied in Table Talk (and XTB). Building Up includes some additional questions which reinforce the main teaching point, apply the teaching more directly or follow up any difficult issues raised by the passage.

Linking with *XTB*

The **XTB** children's notes are based on the same passages as **Table Talk**. There are a number of ways in which you can link the two together:
- Children do **XTB** on their own. Parents then follow these up later (see suggestions below).
- A child and adult work through **XTB** together.
- A family uses **Table Talk** together at breakfast. Older children then use **XTB** on their own later.
- You use **Table Talk** on its own, with no link to **XTB**.

FOLLOWING UP XTB

If your child uses **XTB** on their own it can be helpful to ask them later to show you (or tell you) what they've done. Some useful starter questions are:

- Can you tell me what the reading was about?

- Is there anything you didn't understand or want to ask about?

- Did anything surprise you in the reading? Was there anything that would have surprised the people who first saw it or read about it?

- What did you learn about God, Jesus or the Holy Spirit?

- Is there anything you're going to do as a result of reading this passage?

Table Talk is deliberately not too ambitious. Most families find it quite hard to set up a regular pattern of reading the Bible together—and when they do meet, time is often short. So **Table Talk** is designed to be quick and easy to use, needing little in the way of extra materials, apart from pen and paper now and then.

BUT!!

Most families have special times when they **can** be more ambitious, or do have some extra time available. Here are some suggestions for how you can use **Table Talk** as the basis for a special family adventure...

PICNIC
Take Table Talk with you on a family picnic. Thank God for His beautiful Creation.

WALK
Go for a walk together. Stop somewhere with a good view and read Genesis 1v1—2v4.

GETTING TOGETHER
Invite another family for a meal, and to read the Bible together. The children could make a poster based on the passage.

MUSEUM
Visit a museum to see a display from Bible times. Use it to remind yourselves that the Bible tells us about real people and real history.

HOLIDAYS
Set aside a special time each day while on holiday. Choose some unusual places to read the Bible together—on the beach, up a mountain, in a boat... Take some photos to put on your Table Talk display when you get back from holiday.

You could try one of the special holiday editions of XTB and Table Talk—**Christmas Unpacked**, **Easter Unscrambled** and **Summer Signposts**.

Have an
adventure!

FOOD!
Eat some food linked with the passage you are studying. For example Manna (biscuits made with honey, Exodus 16v31), Unleavened bread or Honeycomb (Matthew 3v4— but don't try the locusts!)

DISPLAY AREA
We find it easier to remember and understand what we learn when we have something to look at. Make a Table Talk display area, for pictures, Bible verses and prayers. Add to it regularly.

VIDEO
A wide range of Bible videos are available—from simple cartoon stories, to whole Gospels filmed with real life actors. (Your local Christian bookshop should have a range.) Choose one that ties in with the passages you are reading together. **Note:** Use the video **in addition** to the Bible passage, not **instead** of it!

PRAYER DIARY
As a special project, make a family prayer diary. Use it to keep a note of things you pray for—and the answers God gives you. This can be a tremendous help to children (and parents!) to learn to trust God in prayer as we see how he answers over time.

Go on—try it!

DRAMA OR PUPPETS
Take time to dramatise a Bible story. Maybe act it out (with costumes if possible) or make some simple puppets to retell the story.

Enough of the introduction, let's get going...

THE BOOK OF ACTS

The key to Acts is found in Jesus' words in Acts 1v8:

"But when the Holy Spirit comes upon you, you will be filled with power, and you will be witnesses for me in Jerusalem, in all Judea and Samaria, and to the ends of the earth."

The rest of Acts is the story of 1v8 coming true, as Jesus' followers tell other people about Him—first in **Jerusalem**, then in **Judea** and **Samaria**, and then further and further...

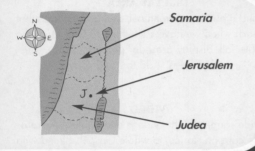

PAUL'S STORY

Acts tells us all about Paul. At the start Paul *didn't believe* that Jesus was the Son of God. He *hated* Christians, and did everything he could to have them stopped.

But then Paul himself was stopped—by Jesus! He discovered that Jesus really is **God's Son**, and Paul became a Christian too. From then on, Paul told everyone he could all about Jesus.

PAUL'S JOURNEY TO ROME (Day 3)

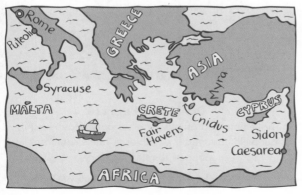

> **KEYPOINT**
> Jesus told Paul that he would go to Rome to tell people there the good news about Jesus.

Today's passages are:
Table Talk: Acts 23v11
XTB: Acts 23v11

TABLE TALK

Draw a picture of **Paul** (a stick man is fine). Read *Paul's Story* in **Notes for Parents**. Add words or drawings to your picture of Paul to sum up what you've read.

Paul went on three long journeys to tell people about Jesus. He mostly walked, but sometimes went by boat. The Jewish leaders **hated** what Paul was teaching about Jesus. When Paul returned to Jerusalem they had him arrested, and put in chains. (*Add more pictures.*)

READ

It looked like the end of the road for Paul. But Jesus had a special message for him. **Read Acts 23v11**

TALK

Where had Paul already spoken (testified/witnessed) about Jesus? (*Jerusalem*) Where else would he speak about Jesus? (*Rome*)

Do you know what country Rome is in? (*Italy*) **Find it on the map opposite**.

THINK

Today, the message about Jesus has spread far further than Rome. It has spread to every country in the world—including yours!

PRAY

Thank God that the message about Jesus has spread to you too. Ask Him to help you to learn more about Jesus as you read the book of Acts together.

Building up

Read Acts 1v8. How far did Jesus say that the message about Him would spread? (*To the ends of the earth.*) Has this promise come true? (*Yes!*) Pray for anyone you know who tells people about Jesus in other countries.

DAY 2
Chain gang

Today's passages are:
Table Talk: Acts 26v28-32
XTB: Acts 26v28-32

TABLE TALK

Where has Jesus promised that Paul will go? (*Rome*) But first, Paul is put on trial in front of three powerful men. Play *Hangman* to discover their names. (*Felix, Festus* and *Agrippa*.)

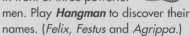

READ

Felix was the Roman Governor, He left Paul in prison for two years! He then handed Paul over to **Festus**, the new Governor. But Festus didn't know what to do with Paul, so he passed him on to **King Agrippa**. Paul told Agrippa all about Jesus. **Read Acts 26v28-32**

TALK

Paul said he wanted Agrippa and the others to be **just like him**—except for **one** thing! What? (v29) (*His chains!*) What did Paul mean? (*That they become Christians too.*) Did Paul deserve to stay in prison? (v31) (*No*) Why couldn't Paul be set free? (v32) (*He'd appealed to have his trial before Caesar.*)

Caesar was the Roman Emperor. Now Paul would go to **Rome**, just as Jesus had promised him!

PRAY

Paul told people about Jesus whenever he could—even when chained up in prison! Are **you** like that? Do you talk about Jesus whenever you can? Do you want to? Pray together about your answers.

Building up
Find out more about the trials before Felix and Festus in **Acts 24v24 – 25v12**. Felix, Festus and Agrippa were all powerful men. But in the end they simply did the will of someone far more powerful! Thank God that **His** plans always work out.

DAY 3
Stormy times

Today's passages are:
Table Talk: Acts 27v13-20
XTB: Acts 27v1-20

TABLE TALK

Paul was sent by ship to the Emperor in Rome. *Draw in his route on the map opposite as you read where they went:*

The ship left **Caesarea** and sailed up the coast to **Sidon**. Then they headed out to sea, passed to the *north* of **Cyprus**, and arrived in **Myra**. At Myra they changed ships, and set off slowly along the coast to **Cnidus**. Then they crossed over to **Crete**, finally stopping at the safe harbour of **Fair Havens**. (*You can read about this voyage in Acts 27v1-8.*)

READ

They'd sailed over 2000 miles. By now it was a bad time of year to sail, but they decided to sail just a bit further. It was a *bad* decision! *Close your eyes and imagine being on the ship as the story is read out.* **Read Acts 27v13-20**

TALK

What did the sailors do to try to save the ship? (*v16—tied down the lifeboat; v17—held the ship together with ropes and lowered the sail; v18-19—threw the cargo and ship's equipment overboard.*) But then what did they do? (v20) (*Gave up hope of being saved.*)

PRAY

The sailors could do nothing more to save themselves—so they gave up hope. But **God** was going to save them all. Thank God that we *never* need to give up hope, if we have put our trust in Him.

Building up
Read Psalm 100. What does this psalm tell us about God? This is our wonderful God, in whom we can **always** trust. Thank Him that "His faithfulness lasts for ever." (v5)

DAY 4
Hopeless hope?

Today's passages are:
Table Talk: Acts 27v21-26
XTB: Acts 27v21-26

TABLE TALK

Talk about any times you have been in a boat—large or small. Were you ever scared? If not, when *might* you be frightened in a boat?

READ

Paul's ship was in a terrible storm. The sailors had given up hope of being saved. But Paul had a message from God...
Read Acts 27v21-26

TALK

What **will** be lost? (v22) (*The ship.*) What **won't** be lost? (v22) (*Any lives.*) What three things did the angel tell Paul? (v24) (*Don't be afraid. You must stand before the Emperor. God will save all on the ship.*) Where would they land? (v26) (*On an island.*)

THINK

Read v25 again. The ship was wrecked and the storm still raging—so why was Paul so confident? Do you think it was easy for him to trust God? Why/why not?

PRAY

Paul knew that God is **far** more powerful than a storm! What are some of the things you are afraid of? (*eg: bullies, debt, war...*) God is **much** more powerful than any of these things. Ask God to help you to trust Him to look after you, no matter what you have to go through.

Building up
Read another stormy story in **Mark 4v35-41**. Jesus was far more powerful than this storm. When the disciples realised this, how did they feel? (v41) (*Terrified*) How would **you** answer their question in v41?

DAY 5
No wrecking God's plans!

Today's passages are:
Table Talk: Acts 27v37-44
XTB: Acts 27v27-44

TABLE TALK

Recap the story so far: Where has Jesus told Paul that he will go? (*Rome*) What's happened to the ship? (*It was caught in a storm.*) What has God promised? (*No lives will be lost.*)

Read the cartoon story opposite to find out what happened next.

READ

If you have **older children**, read the whole story in **Acts 27v27-44**, and include the questions in *Building Up*.

With **younger children** just read **Acts 27v37-44**.

TALK

How many people were on board? (v37) (*276*) What did the ship land on? (v41) (*A sandbank.*) The soldiers tried to kill the prisoners, to stop them escaping. Who stopped them? (v42) (*The Roman Centurion.*) How many people were saved? (v44) (*All 276 of them!*)

THINK

This was a terrible storm. The ship was completely destroyed. So why was nobody killed? (*Because God kept His promise to save them all.*)

PRAY

Nothing can wreck God's plans! Thank God that He always keeps His promises.

Building up
Read Acts 27v27-44. This passage is summarised in the cartoon strip, but did you notice that the writer puts "we" in v27 and "us" in v37. He was on the ship too! Who is he? (*Luke, who also wrote Luke's Gospel. See Acts 1v1.*)

DAY 5
Notes for Parents

STORM AT SEA

The ship had been tossed around by the storm for **two weeks!** God had promised to save everyone on board, but they still had to reach land...

The sailors felt they were close to land – so they checked how deep the sea was.

At first...

It's 120 feet deep.

But then...

Now it's only 90 feet deep!

The sailors let down the lifeboat.

We're going to put out some anchors.

But really they were planning to...

ESCAPE!

Paul knew what was happening.

Unless they stay on board, we can't be saved!

So the soldiers cut the ropes, and set the lifeboat free

Then Paul spoke to everyone.

You haven't eaten for 14 days.

Now eat some food. You need it to survive.

Paul thanked God for the food...

...and they all ate.

DAY 6
Snakes alive

KEYPOINT
God kept Paul safe from shipwreck and snakebite, so that he could go to Rome.

Today's passages are:
Table Talk: Acts 28v1-6
XTB: Acts 28v1-10

TABLE TALK

The ship was wrecked, but the people were all safe. They landed on the island of **Malta**. *Find Malta on the map on Day 1. Draw their route from Crete to Malta.*

READ

The local islanders welcomed them warmly. But as Paul collected wood for the fire, something very surprising happened. **Read Acts 28v1-6**

TALK

What happened as Paul collected the wood? (v3) (*A snake fastened itself on his hand.*) What did the islanders think this meant? (v4) (*That Paul was a murderer.*) Did the snake hurt Paul? (v5) (*No*) Then the islanders changed their minds. Now who did they think Paul was? (v6) (*A god!*)

THINK

Paul wasn't a murderer or a god! Who do you think kept Paul safe from the snake? (*God did.*) Why? (*So that Paul would go to Rome as God promised.*)

PRAY

Do you know anyone who travels to tell people about Jesus? (*Maybe a missionary, or someone from your church.*) Ask God to keep them safe as they travel.

Building up

Read Acts 28v7-10 Paul wasn't a murderer or a god. But he was a servant of the **one true God** (as he had told his fellow travellers in Acts 27v23). When Paul found that the chief official's father was ill, what did he do? (v8) (*Prayed, and put his hands on him.*) How many of the sick islanders were healed? (v9) (*All of them.*)

DAY 7
Rome at last

Today's passages are:
Table Talk: Acts 28v11-16
XTB: Acts 28v11-16

 TABLE TALK
Look again at the map on Day 1. Paul is still heading for Rome. Where do you think he will stop on the way? (*Starting from Malta.*)

 READ
Look out for these places as you read the passage. **Read Acts 28v11-16**

 Draw the route from Malta to Rome.

 TALK

How long had they stayed on Malta? (v11) (*Three months.*) Who did they meet in Puteoli? (v14) (*Some Christians.*) How long did they stay with these Christians? (*A week.*) What did the Christians in Rome do when they heard about Paul? (v15) (*They came to meet him.*) How did Paul react? (v15) (*He thanked God and was encouraged.*)

 THINK
The Christians from Rome walked over 40 miles to meet Paul. No wonder Paul was encouraged! Think of someone you know who needs encouraging. (Perhaps they are ill, sad or lonely.) How can you encourage them this week? (*A phone call, a visit, a present...*)

 PRAY
Pray for this person and ask God to help you to encourage them. Tell them that you are praying for them, too.

Building up
Different Bible versions translate v14-15 as "believers" or "brothers". Why are these good names for Christians? [*Christians **believe** that Jesus died for them—see John 3v16. Christians are members of God's family, they are **brothers** and **sisters** in Christ—see Hebrews 2v11.*]

DAY 8
The hope of Israel

Today's passages are:
Table Talk: Acts 28v23-24
XTB: Acts 28v17-24

TABLE TALK
Paul has arrived in Rome, and is now in chains, guarded by a Roman soldier. How would **you** feel, if you were Paul?

READ
Paul called the Jewish leaders to see him. He told them he had done nothing wrong. He said, "It is because of *the hope of Israel* that I am in chains." (v20) The Jewish leaders wanted to know more, so they arranged to come and see him again. **Read Acts 28v23-24**

TALK
What kingdom did Paul tell them about? (v23) (*The kingdom of God.*) What did Paul quote? (v23) (*The Law of Moses and the Prophets, which means the Old Testament.*) Did they believe Paul? (v24) (*Some did, others didn't.*)

THINK
"The hope of Israel" means the Jewish hope that God would keep His promise to send them a new King (called the Christ). Paul used the Old Testament to show them that **Jesus** was this promised King.

PRAY
Jesus wasn't just "the hope of Israel". He is the hope of the **whole world**. (*We'll find out more on Day 10.*) Thank God for sending Jesus as our King.

Building up
Read Acts 28v16-22 Had Paul done anything against Jewish customs? Or against the Romans? (*No—see v17-18.*) But Paul didn't complain about being in chains. Why not? What *did* Paul talk about? (See v20) Ask God to help *you* to take every opportunity to talk about Jesus, even when things are hard or unfair.

Looking without seeing

Notes for Parents

KEYPOINT
The great news about Jesus is for everyone.

Today's passages are:
Table Talk: Acts 28v24-28
XTB: Acts 28v24-28

TABLE TALK

If you can, speak to your child in a foreign language—or tune in to a foreign radio station. Sometimes we can *listen*, but not *understand*, because we don't know the language. The people listening to Paul understood his language—but they wouldn't *really listen* to what he was telling them about Jesus.

READ

Read Acts 28v24-28

TALK

Who was Paul quoting? (v25) (*Isaiah, an Old Testament writer.*) Paul was saying that the Jewish leaders had *listened*, but they hadn't really *heard* him! They'd *looked* without *seeing*. Most of them still refused to believe the truth about Jesus. Who did Paul say the good news about Jesus would be sent to? (v28) (*The Gentiles [non-Jews]*). Would *they* listen? (*Yes!*)

WOW!

The great news about Jesus is for **everyone**—for Jews *and* Gentiles. That includes you!

PRAY

Thank God that the good news about Jesus is for everyone. Pray for anyone who tells **you** about Jesus. Ask God to help them.

Building up

Isaiah lived more than 700 years before Paul. He spoke these words to the Jewish people of his time. Read them for yourself in **Isaiah 6v8-10**. Isaiah's message was a hard one. But thank God that some people *do* listen and understand—because **God** opens their ears. Thank God for anyone you know who has recently joined your church or become a Christian.

GOD'S RESCUE PLAN

(You need pencil & paper.) *Prepare three separate pieces of paper. Write **GOD** on one, **SIN** on a second, and draw a person (a stick man is fine) on the third.*

Place the pieces of paper as shown.

ASK: *WHAT IS SIN?*
Sin is more than just doing wrong things. We all like to be **in charge** of our own lives. We do what **we** want instead of what **God** wants. This is called Sin.

ASK: *WHAT DOES SIN DO?*
As the picture shows, **sin** gets in the way between us and God. It stops us from knowing God and from being His friends. Sin is a H-U-G-E problem—and there is nothing **we** can do about it.

But the great news is that Jesus came as our Rescuer, to ***save*** us from our sin. When Jesus died on the cross He was being punished. He took the punishment that we deserve, so that we can be forgiven.

Take the paper saying SIN and tear it in half. Then place the two halves as shown.

ASK: *WHAT GETS IN THE WAY NOW BETWEEN PEOPLE AND GOD?*
(Answer: *Nothing!*)

When Jesus died, He dealt with the problem of sin so that we can be forgiven. There is **nothing** to separate us from God any more. This was **God's Rescue Plan** for us. It shows why "***God saves***" is such a great title for Jesus.

DAY 10
To boldly teach...

KEYPOINT
For the next two years, Paul carried on teaching boldly about Jesus, God's chosen King.

Today's passages are:
Table Talk: Acts 28v30-31
XTB: Acts 28v30-31

TABLE TALK

Imagine not being allowed to leave your house—for **two years!** How would you feel? What would you find hardest?

READ

For the next two years, Paul lived in his own rented house. He was still in chains, guarded by a Roman soldier, but anyone could come and visit him.
Read Acts 28v30-31

TALK

How did Paul respond to his visitors? (v30) (*He welcomed them all.*) Who did he tell them about? (v31) (*The Lord Jesus Christ.*)

THINK

The name **Jesus** means "*God saves*". Why is this a good name for Jesus? (*It tells us who He is—God, and what He does—He saves us.*)

DO

Use the illustration in **Notes for Parents** (*on the previous page*) to show how Jesus saves us from our sins.

The name **Christ** means "*God's chosen King*". Jesus didn't just come as our Rescuer. He also came as King. Not a king who lives in a palace, but King of our lives.

PRAY

Is Jesus **your** Rescuer and King? Do you want Him to be? Do you want to tell your friends about Him like Paul did? Pray together about your answers.

Building up
Look back to **Acts 1v8**, the key verse for the book of Acts. All the way through Acts, we see that God's message about Jesus **can't be stopped**. At the end of Acts, Paul is in chains. But he is totally **free** to teach about Jesus, and does so **boldly**. Thank God that the great news about Jesus is for everyone, and that it can't be stopped.

DAY 11
Paul's prison post

KEYPOINT
Paul said it was a good thing to be in chains, because the news about Jesus was spread.

Today's passages are:
Table Talk: Philippians 1v12-14
XTB: Philippians 1v12-14

TABLE TALK

Collect up some recent post. Who is it from and what is it about? (*Personal letters, bills, junk mail...*) Paul was in chains in Rome, but he was free to write **letters**. Do you think his letters were like the post you've just looked at? What do you think Paul wrote about?

READ

We're going to dip into three letters Paul wrote from prison. He wrote **Philippians** to the Christians who lived in the city of Philippi, in northern Greece. In it, he wrote something surprising about being in chains... **Read Philippians 1v12-14**

TALK

Wow! Paul is saying that it's a **good** thing that he is in prison! Find two reasons why. (*v13—the whole palace guard knew that Paul was in chains for Jesus Christ; v14—other Christians were encouraged to talk about Jesus fearlessly.*)

THINK

Paul took every opportunity to talk to people about Jesus. Every time another soldier was put on guard duty, Paul had someone new to talk with about Jesus. Each guard was a captive audience!

PRAY

How about you? How do you react when things get tough? Do you grumble? Or do you ask God to show you ways to keep serving Him? Pray together about your answers.

Building up
Philippians is sometimes known as "the rejoicing letter". Have a flick through to spot some of the places where Paul writes about joy or rejoicing. (*eg: 1v4, 1v18, 2v18, 3v1, 4v10 and many more...*) **Who** are they to rejoice in? (*See Phil 4v4*) Spend some time rejoicing in the Lord together. Thank Him for loving you, and maybe even sing together.

DAY 12
Rejoice

KEYPOINT
Paul told his readers to always rejoice in the Lord.

Today's passages are:
Table Talk: Philippians 4v4
XTB: Philippians 4v4

TABLE TALK

Look up "rejoice" in a dictionary.

READ

Paul was in prison, but he still told those reading his letter that they were to rejoice! **Read Philippians 4v4**

Who did Paul tell the Philippians to rejoice in? (*The Lord.*)

DO

Copy Philippians 4v4 onto a large sheet of paper. Draw rejoicing pictures around it (*eg: happy faces, stars, trumpets...*) While you're making the poster, learn this verse as a Memory Verse. Test each other several times during the day.

THINK

Paul didn't just rejoice when things were going well. He even rejoiced in prison! If you are a Christian, then there are some great reasons to rejoice (*even when things seem hard*). Here are some:

- God loves you.
- God always listens to your prayers.
- Jesus died for you.
- Jesus wants you to be His friend.

PRAY

Choose some (or all!) of these to thank God for.

You may know a song based on this verse. If so, sing it together.

Building up
When Paul had first visited Philippi, he ended up being whipped and thrown into prison! But he hadn't grumbled or sulked. Instead, he was *singing*—rejoicing in the Lord! Find out more in **Acts 16v25-34**.

DAY 13
Open door

KEYPOINT
Paul needed God to open a door for the message about Jesus to be heard.

Today's passages are:
Table Talk: Colossians 4v2-4
XTB: Colossians 4v2-4

TABLE TALK

Today's Table Talk is about opening closed doors. **Close** door of your room. If there's space, all sit on the floor by the door as you do Table Talk.

Philippians wasn't the only letter Paul wrote from prison. He also wrote to the Christians in the city of **Colossae** (in modern-day Turkey).
Read Colossians 4v2-4

READ

TALK

What did Paul tell his readers to keep doing? (v2) (*Praying*) Paul needed God to "open a door". (Some Bibles translate this as "give a good opportunity".) What did God need to open a door for? (v3) (*The message about Jesus. See **Building Up** below if you want to know more about why Paul calls it "the mystery of Christ".*) What else did Paul need prayer for? (v4) (*That God would help Paul to talk **clearly** about Jesus.*)

DO

Now **open** the door to your room.

PRAY

Think of someone you know who tells other people about Jesus. Pray these same two things for them—that God will **open a door** for them to talk to others, and that He will help them to talk about Jesus **clearly**.

Building up
Paul writes about "the mystery of Christ" in v3. This doesn't mean that it's a secret! But we can **only** know the truth about Jesus because **God** makes it known to us. If God didn't show us who Jesus really is, it would stay a mystery. Thank God for showing you the truth about Jesus.

Salt and...

So much more

KEYPOINT
Paul told the Colossians that their conversation should be "seasoned with salt".

Today's passages are:
Table Talk: Colossians 4v5-6
XTB: Colossians 4v5-6

KEYPOINT
Paul told the Ephesians how great God is, and how He is able to do far more than they imagine.

Today's passages are:
Table Talk: Ephesians 3v20-21
XTB: Ephesians 3v20-21

TABLE TALK

Sprinkle a little salt on your finger and taste it. What do you add salt to? (*I like it on popcorn and porridge!*)

READ

In yesterday's reading, what did Paul ask the Colossians to pray for? (*An open door.*) Now Paul wants the Colossians to be *salty*! **Read Colossians 4v5-6**

THINK

Different Bible versions use various ways to explain what Paul is saying in verse 6. A good translation is, "Let your speech always be gracious, seasoned with salt." Salt makes a huge **difference** to food. (Think of fish and chips!)

Too little salt can be boring.

Too much can make you sick!

What do you think it means to "season your speech with salt"? (*When you talk with your friends, being a Christian should make a **difference** to what you say. You don't want to be like a boring chip! You want to say interesting things about Jesus.*)

PRAY

Do you want to talk with your friends about Jesus? If so, pray Paul's prayer: "Dear God, please open a door for me to talk about Jesus, and let what I say be salty. Amen"

Building up
As well as being salty, our conversation should be "full of grace" (v6). What is God's **grace**? (*It is the undeserved kindness of God.*) God offers us the undeserved gift of forgiveness through Jesus' death for us. So, if our conversation is to be "full of grace", that means full of **Jesus**.

TABLE TALK

Can you remember the Memory Verse from Day 12? (Each take turns to say it.)

READ

Our last dip into Paul's prison letters is in the book of **Ephesians**. When I was a student, I helped with a Beach Mission in the south of England. The whole team were told to learn these verses before we came. **Read Ephesians 3v20-21**

TALK

What does Paul say that God is able to do? (v20) (*So much more than we ask, or even imagine!*) What difference should this make to our prayers?

I have a sign above my door. It says, "God is able." It reminds me that God is able to answer all my prayers, and that **nothing** is too hard for Him.

DO

(*Optional*) Write "**God is able**" on a sticky note. Put it where you will see it when you pray.

The Beach Mission's aim was to tell holiday-makers about Jesus. That was scary! But our Memory Verse reminded us that God was able to answer all our prayers, and to do far more than we could even think of. And He did!

PRAY

God is able to answer all *your* prayers too. Talk to God about anything you are scared, worried, happy or sad about. Then read **v20-21** again, and praise God for being so great!

Building up
It's true that God is always *able* to answer our prayers. But sometimes His answer is "No" or "Wait". God always knows what's best for us, so He knows the best way to answer our prayers too. Thank Him that you can always trust Him to give good answers.

EXTRAORDINARY EXODUS

The first half of Exodus show how God rescued the Israelites from Egypt...

The Israelites had lived in Egypt for 400 years.

God chose Moses to be their leader and rescue them

God had a message for Pharaoh, the king of Egypt.

Let my people go so that they may worship me.

But Pharaoh refused.

I do not know the LORD.

I will not let Israel go!

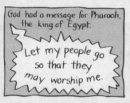

So God sent ten terrible plagues on Egypt.

After the last plague, (the Passover), Pharaoh let the Israelites go.

Then Pharaoh changed his mind and chased after them

But God made a dry path through the Red Sea...

...and the Israelites escaped.

They were safe at last!

KEYPOINT
God has rescued the Israelites They must remember what He's done, and trust Him.

Today's passages are:
Table Talk: Exodus 13v8-10
XTB: Exodus 13v8-10

TABLE TALK

Use the cartoon story in **Notes for Parents** to recap the first half of Exodus.

READ

God had done *amazing* things for the Israelites. Now they needed to *remember* what God had done for them, and *trust* Him for the future. But God knew that their memories would easily become "forgetories"—so He gave them a way of remembering how He had rescued them from Egypt. Each year, they were to hold a special festival.
Read Exodus 13v8-10

TALK

During the festival they ate bread without yeast (unleavened bread), just as they had when they escaped from Egypt. What did the festival remind them of? (v9) (*To remember God's law, and that God had rescued them from Egypt.*)

DO

All through the Bible, God's people are told to *remember* what God has done for them. Copy today's Memory Verse onto some paper, and learn it together. **"Praise the Lord, O my soul, and do not forget how kind He is."** Psalm 103v2

PRAY

Remember some of the great things God has done for you. Ask Him to help you never to forget how great He is, and all that He has done for you.

Building up
When the Israelites fled from Egypt, they took unleavened dough with them. Find out more in **Exodus 12v33-39**.

DAY 17
Sweet and sour

 TABLE TALK

Pour a glass of water and taste it. Do you know how clean water gets to your home? (*eg: rain water, to rivers, to reservoir, to water purification plant, via pipes and stopcocks to your tap.*)

 READ

In Exodus 15, the Israelites have just safely crossed the Red Sea. Now they're travelling through the desert. But they've walked three days without finding water. Do you think they will *trust* God? Or start *grumbling*? Find out in **Exodus 15v22-25a** (*ie: the first part of verse 25*)

 TALK

Why couldn't they drink the water at Marah? (v23) (*It was too bitter.*) Did they trust God or grumble? (v24) (*Grumbled*) How did God make the water sweet for them? (v25) (*He showed Moses some wood to throw in.*)

 THINK

The Israelites *grumbled*—but why should they have *trusted*? (*They should have remembered all that God had done for them.*) The Israelites needed to be **trusters**, not **grumblers**. What about you? Are you trusters? Or grumblers?

 PRAY

Say yesterday's Memory Verse together. Ask God to help you to be a truster, not a grumbler.

Building up
Read what happened next in **Exodus 15v25b-27**. How were the Israelites to behave if they wanted God to take care of them? (v26) (*Trust and obey Him.*) The way to show they **trusted** God was by **obeying** Him. That's true for us too. If we really trust God, we will obey all His commands. Pray together about this.

DAY 18 Trusters or grumblers?

 TABLE TALK

Table Talk Test: Ask your child some questions about *Exodus*. eg: Who did God choose to lead the Israelites? How many plagues were there? Which sea did the Israelites cross? What happened in yesterday's story at Marah?

 READ

In school, teachers *test* us to find out what we've learned. In today's story, **God** sets a test for the Israelites. The test will show whether they've learned to trust Him at last. **Read Exodus 16v1-5**

 TALK

Were the Israelites trusters or grumblers? (v2) (*Grumblers*) How did they describe living in Egypt? (*See v3*) They had *forgotten* what it was like to be slaves, and *forgotten* all that God had done for them! God could have been very angry. But instead, what did He promise them? (v4) (*Bread from heaven.*) He also set them a **test**. What would the test show? (v4) (*If they'd follow His instructions.*)

 THINK

The way to show that they *trusted* God, was by *obeying* God—following His instructions. Do you think they will? Why/why not? (*We'll find out in the next few days.*)

 PRAY

For **us** too, the way to show we *trust* God is by *obeying* Him. Do you want to trust and obey God? Ask Him to help you.

Building up
Jesus told His followers, "You are my friends if you do what I command you." Read the whole passage in **John 15v12-17**. Ask Jesus to help you to obey His command to "love each other".

DAY 19
What is it?

TABLE TALK

How many types of food can you think of that begin with "M"? (*eg: milk, melon, meat, mints, marshmallows, mushrooms, Mars bars!*)

READ

Moses and Aaron had a message for the Israelites from God. He promised to give them food in the desert, so that they will know that He is **their God**, who rescued them from Egypt.
Read Exodus 16v11-15

TALK

What will God give them at twilight? (v12) (*Meat*) And in the morning? (*Bread*) What will that show the Israelites? (v12) (*That He is the Lord their God.*) What did God send for meat? (v13) (*Quail, a small bird.*) What did the "bread" look like? (*See v14*) Jump ahead to **v31** to find out what they called this bread, and what it tasted like. (*Manna means "What is it?".*)

Did God keep His promise to give food to the Israelites? (*Yes*)

PRAY

Thank God that He *always* keeps His promises.

Building up
Read Exodus 16v6-10 What do these verses tell us about God? What do they tell us about the Israelites? Do you think the Israelites will change? Do you think God will?

DAY 20
Manna manners

DO

Find something that holds about two litres. (*A cola bottle, a measuring jug...*)

READ

As we saw on Day 18, God gave the Israelites a **test**, to find out if they would follow His instructions. His instructions for collecting the manna were very clear. They were to collect an **omer** of manna each. (An omer is about two litres.) This was just enough for one day.
Read Exodus 16v16-20

TALK

The Israelites collected the manna as they were told. But what were they told *not* to do? (v19) (*Not to keep any for tomorrow.*) God had promised to give them food *every day* (v4-5). If they **trusted** Him, they didn't need to keep any extra for tomorrow. But some of the people *didn't* trust God. What did they do? (v20) (*Kept some of the manna.*) What happened to the manna they kept? (v20) (*It was full of maggots!*)

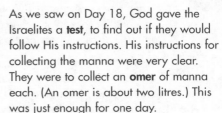

THINK

Even though God had done **so much** for the Israelites, some of them still found it hard to trust Him. Do *you* find it hard to trust God sometimes? When?

PRAY

Ask God to help you to keep trusting Him every day.

Building up
God provided manna for the Israelites for the next 40 years! Imagine being an Israelite, collecting manna each morning. What do you think it would show you about God? (*eg: That He cares for your needs, that He can provide food in the desert, that He keeps His promises.*)

DAY 21 More manna manners

KEYPOINT
The Israelites were to collect twice as much manna on Day 6, and then rest on Day 7.

Today's passages are:
Table Talk: Exodus 16v21-27
XTB: Exodus 16v21-30

TABLE TALK

Recap: How much manna were the Israelites to collect each day? (*Enough for one day—an omer/two litres.*) What happened if they kept it for the next day? (*It was full of maggots!*)

This was the pattern for five days of the week. But it changed on Day Six. Look back to **Exodus 16v5** to see what God said they should do then. (*Collect twice as much as usual.*)

READ

The seventh day (the Sabbath) was a day of rest. God told them **not** to collect manna on the Sabbath—there would be nothing there! Do you think the Israelites will keep God's instructions this time? Read **Exodus 16v21-27** to find out.

TALK

How much did the people collect on the sixth day? (v22) (*Two omers/four litres.*) Usually any extra went rotten overnight. But what happened this time? (v24) (*It stayed fresh.*) Did all of the Israelites follow God's instructions? (v27) (*No, some went looking on the Sabbath too.*)

PRAY

The Israelites keep letting God down. Are *you* sometimes like that too? Think carefully about times when you have let God down. Say sorry for disobeying Him, and ask Him to help you change.

Building up
Read Exodus 16v27-30 How much manna did God provide on the sixth day? (*Enough for two days.*) Why? (*Because the seventh day is to be a day of rest.*) The day of rest is to be a regular pattern for the Israelites. We will find out more about it on Day 52. (The Ten Commandments)

DAY 22 Remember not to forget!

KEYPOINT
The Israelites were to keep a jar of manna to remind them how God had fed them in the desert.

Today's passages are:
Table Talk: Exodus 16v31-36
XTB: Exodus 16v31-36

TABLE TALK

How do you remember things? (eg: *note on the fridge door, family calendar...*) Collect some examples.

READ

We've seen how the Israelites keep *forgetting* how great God has been to them. So God tells Moses to do something to remind them in the future. **Read Exodus 16v31-36**

What did manna taste like? (*Honey wafers.*)

DO

If possible, each have a spoonful of honey to taste.

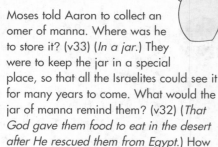

Moses told Aaron to collect an omer of manna. Where was he to store it? (v33) (*In a jar.*) They were to keep the jar in a special place, so that all the Israelites could see it for many years to come. What would the jar of manna remind them? (v32) (*That God gave them food to eat in the desert after He rescued them from Egypt.*) How long did God give them manna for? (v35) (*40 years!*)

PRAY

Do you remember the Memory Verses from Days 12 and 16? Say them together, and thank God for all He has given you.

Building up
Do you know The Lord's Prayer? One part says, "Give us today our daily bread." God doesn't look after us on some days and then forget us on others! God gives us what we need *every day*. (Just like He gave the Israelites manna for every day.) Thank God that He is like this—and maybe say The Lord's Prayer together.

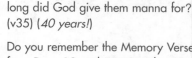

DAY 23
Spot the difference?

Today's passages are:
Table Talk: Exodus 17v1-7
XTB: Exodus 17v1-7

TABLE TALK

See if you can sound like a large crowd of grumbling people! Start quietly ("Mutter, mutter"), get louder ("Grumble, grumble", "It's not fair!") and then quieten down again.

READ

This is what the Israelites were like at *Marah* (Day 17) when there was no water to drink. But even though they grumbled, God gave them the water they needed. Since then, He has also given them quail and manna to eat. But now, at *Rephidim*, the Israelites again have no water. Do you think they will *trust* God this time? Or *grumble*? **Read Exodus 17v1-7**

TALK

Did the people trust or grumble? (*Grumble*) What shocking thing did they accuse Moses (and God!) of planning? (v3) (*That they were brought out of Egypt to be killed.*) Who did Moses turn to for help? (v4) (*God*) How did God provide water? (*See v5-6*)

Draw what happened.

THINK

Spot the difference between Moses and the other Israelites. What did the Israelites do when they faced trouble? (*Grumble*) What did Moses do? (*Turn to God for help.*) What do *you* do when things are hard? Grumble? Or ask God for help? Pray together about your answers.

PRAY

Building up
Read v7 again. How would you answer their question, "Is the Lord with us or not?" (*What evidence have you read in Exodus? Look back at God's promise in Ex 6v6-8.*)

DAY 24
Arms for the army

Today's passages are:
Table Talk: Exodus 17v8-13
XTB: Exodus 17v8-13

TABLE TALK

Where do you usually pray? Are there any unusual places you have prayed in? In Bible times people often stood to pray with their hands held up high. Moses prays like this in today's story, at the top of a hill.

READ

The Amalekites were a fierce race of people. They attacked the Israelites at Rephidim. **Read Exodus 17v8-13**

TALK

Who led the Israelite army? (v10) (*Joshua—He doesn't know it yet, but he will be the next leader of the Israelites after Moses.*) Who won when Moses prayed? (v11) (*The Israelites.*) Who won when Moses put his hands down and stopped praying? (*The Amalekites.*) How did Aaron and Hur help Moses to pray? (*See v12*) Who won the battle? (v13) (*Joshua and the Israelites.*)

THINK

Why do you think the Israelites won? Was it because their army was better? What made the difference? (*Prayer*)

PRAY

We *can* pray with our hands up high, but we don't have to! We can pray standing, sitting, lying down... Move to somewhere you don't usually pray. (*The porch, on the stairs...*) Thank God that you can pray anywhere, anytime. Ask Him to help you to trust Him like Moses did.

Building up
Jesus' disciples asked Him to teach them to pray. Read His answer in **Luke 11v1-13**. Jesus' two stories teach us different things about prayer. *We* should be like the friend at midnight—and *keep on* praying persistently (v8). *God* is like a perfect father. He always gives *good* answers to our prayers (v13).

KEYPOINT
Moses wrote an account of the battle so that God's victory would be remembered.

Today's passages are:
Table Talk: Exodus 17v14-16
XTB: Exodus 17v14-16

The Israelites

TABLE TALK

(*You need pencil and paper.*) Draw the Israelites in the middle of the paper (stick men will do). Round them draw or write some of the things that you've read about in Exodus. (*eg: escape from Egypt, crossing Red Sea, God providing water, quail and manna, battle with Amalekites.*)

READ

All through Exodus, we've seen God do amazing things for the Israelites. We've also seen how easily they *forget* what He's done, and stop trusting Him. They need help to *remember* what God has done.
Read Exodus 17v14-16

TALK

God told Moses to write an account of the victory. Why? (v14) (*So that it would be remembered.*) Moses also built an altar to God. What did he call it? (v15) (*"The Lord is my banner."*) This reminded the Israelites that God was with them, and that He would take care of them and fight for them.

PRAY

How do *you* remind yourselves of what God has done? (*eg: A Table Talk display, a prayer diary...*) Spend some time now remembering what God has done for you. Thank and praise Him.

Building up
Think back over the events in Exodus. What have you learned about God? Thank God that He is always faithful to His people.

THE FINAL PIECE
We're about to look at the last few chapters of Matthew's book about Jesus. Just like the best films, it will involve all our emotions, but also the best ending ever.

But before we get started, let's recap on the story so far...

1 The First Christmas
Jesus is born as the promised King.

2 The Last Three Years of Jesus' Life
Matthew tells us all about Jesus' life: about His miracles, His teaching and His example.

3 Palm Sunday
Jesus rides into Jerusalem on a donkey. The crowds cheer and spread palm branches on the road.

4 The Plot
Not everyone's pleased to see Jesus. The religious leaders finally plot to have Jesus killed.

5 Betrayal
One of Jesus' closest friends is persuaded to turn Jesus over to them to face a death sentence.

6 The Final Piece
Let's see what happens.

DAY 26
A meal to remember

KEYPOINT
We must remember important things God has done for us.

Today's passages are:
Table Talk: Matthew 26v17-19
XTB: Matthew 26v17-19

 TABLE TALK
For the next 20 days we'll be reading the last part of Matthew's book about Jesus. Use **Notes for Parents** to see what the rest of his book tells us.

 THINK
What important events do you celebrate each year? (*Birthdays, Anniversary, Easter, Christmas, New Year*). How many of these are celebrated with a meal of some kind?

 READ
Today, Jesus' disciples get ready for a meal to help them *remember*.
Read Matthew 26v17-19

 TALK
What was this meal called? (v17) (*The Passover meal.*) Jews ate this meal every year to remember that God had rescued them from slavery in Egypt.

 THINK
What did Jesus mean when He said His hour (appointed time) had come? (v18) (*Jesus was going to die soon.*) How did the disciples react to this? (*They seemed to ignore what Jesus said about 'His appointed time', and just got on with preparing for the Passover meal.*)

 DO
What can *you* thank God for? Make a poster with words and drawings to remind you of what He has done for you.

Using your poster, thank God for all the things you have put on it.

 PRAY

Building up
Go back to Day 16 and read again about the Passover Meal when God rescued the Jews from slavery in Egypt.

DAY 27
Some friend

KEYPOINT
God is always in control, even when bad things happen.

Today's passages are:
Table Talk: Matthew 26v20-22 & 25
XTB: Matthew 26v20-25

 TABLE TALK
Have your friends ever let you down? What happened? Talk about how you felt.

Jesus was let down by a close friend.
Read Matthew 26v20-22

 READ
What unexpected announcement did Jesus make? (v21) (*One of the disciples would betray Him.*) How did the disciples react to this sudden news? (*They were sad and wondered who it would be.*)

 TALK
Jesus knew it was **Judas** who would betray Him. **Read verse 25**

How do you think Jesus felt, knowing a close friend would hand Him over to the authorities? Even with this knowledge, Jesus carried on with the meal! He didn't try to stop Judas or run away. Why not? (*He knew everything was happening just as God planned—just as it says in the Old Testament.*)

 THINK
Do *you* believe God is always in control? The Bible says He is and that we need to trust Him. Ask God to help you to always trust Him no matter what happens to you.

PRAY

Building up
The disciples asked a strange question in verse 22. What was it? Were the disciples convinced they were in control of their lives?

Read Matthew 20:17-18. Before Jesus had arrived in Jerusalem, He *knew* what was going to happen to Him. He knew that **God** was in control, even if it would be difficult.

DAY 28
Remembering rescue

Today's passages are:
Table Talk: Matthew 26v26-28
XTB: Matthew 26v26-30

TABLE TALK

Sometimes we do things or keep things to remind us of something that happened in the past. Married couples return to the place where they first met; we keep newspaper cuttings; we buy music, which brings back memories; we keep photographs. Is this true for you? Talk about (and look at) some examples.

READ

As you read the passage, see if you can spot *two things* we use to remember Jesus. **Read Matthew 26v26-28**

TALK

What did Jesus take first, and what did He do with it? (v26) (*Bread, gave thanks, broke it and gave it to them.*) What did He take next and what did He do with it? (v27) (*Cup, gave thanks and gave it to them to drink.*) What did Jesus say the bread and the cup were like? (*His body and blood.*) Why did Jesus say His blood would be poured out? (v28) (*For the forgiveness of sins.*)

DO

(*Optional*) Get some bread and a cup of blackcurrant and act out the passage.

PRAY

Jesus knew that He was going to die to take the punishment for our sins. Thank Jesus for what He did so that your sins could be forgiven.

Building up
Read Paul's account of the Last Supper in **1 Corinthians 11v23-26**. We still remember this meal today. It is sometimes known as The Lord's Supper, Communion or the Eucharist. What does Paul say we are doing when we share bread and wine together? (v26) (*Proclaiming Jesus' death.*)

DAY 29
Trouble ahead

Today's passages are:
Table Talk: Matthew 26v31-35
XTB: Matthew 26v31-35

TABLE TALK

Have you ever thought you would be really brave in a situation and then when it happened got really scared? Talk about some situations where this has happened.

READ

Jesus *knew* what was about to happen to Him. He also knew how His friends would react. **Read Matthew 26v31-35**

TALK

What did Jesus say the disciples would all do? (v31) (*Fall away/run away.*) What did Peter say *he* would do? (v33 & 35) (*Never fall away, "Even if I have to die".*) What about the other disciples? (v35) (*They all said the same.*)

DO

Jesus said that like sheep all His friends would be scattered. **Draw two pictures** showing, a) all the sheep together with the shepherd, b) the shepherd taken and the sheep scattered.

PRAY

It can be hard being Jesus' friend. Are there any situations you find hard at the moment? Ask Jesus to help you.

Building up
Everything happening to Jesus was written in the Old Testament, long before He was born. This is called *prophesy*.
Read Zechariah 13v7, which is also in Matthew 26v31. Who is the shepherd, who are the sheep, and what will happen? Remember **God** is in control—and wait and see. (*And check out the clue in Matthew 26v32!*)

DAY 30
No other way

KEYPOINT
Jesus was prepared even to face God's anger because He loves us so much.

Today's passages are:
Table Talk: Matthew 26v39
XTB: Matthew 26v36-46

TABLE TALK

Write out some funny phrases like, "I slept like a ...." (*log*); "I saw .... before my eyes" (*stars*); "I'm like a .... of ...." (*block of ice*). Draw the missing word and get your children to try to guess the phrase. *Like these phrases, today's story uses an object as a picture of something else.*

READ

Jesus prays about what is about to happen to Him because He doesn't want it to. **Read Matthew 26v39**

TALK

How did Jesus pray? (*Face down.*) What object did Jesus use as a picture? (*A cup.*) What do you think the cup was a picture of? (*All that was about to happen.*)

THINK

Jesus knew that on the cross God the Father would punish Him for our sin. He knew it would be like drinking from a cup full of God's anger.

What did Jesus say at the end of His prayer? (*He wants to do whatever God wants.*)

PRAY

Do you realise how much Jesus went through to rescue you? Thank God for what He did.

Building up
Jesus knew what was about to happen to Him. It was really troubling Him and He was worried. **Read Matthew 26v36-46** What did Jesus do? (*Prayed*) He knew the situation was serious. His first thought was to pray about it. When you are troubled or worried turn to God in prayer first.

DAY 31
No surprises

TABLE TALK

Either: Can you think of situations where you knew what would happen? Share some of them. **Or:** Have a competition to see who's best at looking surprised.

On Day 27 we found out that Jesus *knew* that Judas would betray Him. The time has now come.

READ

In verse 46, Jesus says to His sleepy friends, "Get up, let's go! Here comes my betrayer". Read **Matthew 26v47-56**

TALK

Who came with Judas and what were they carrying? (See v47) How did Judas say they would know who to arrest? (v48) (*The one he kissed.*)

How did the disciples react? (v51) (*They started to fight back.*) Jesus stopped them and showed *He* was in control. What did He say He could do? (v53) (*Call for 12 legions of angels.*)

Why did Jesus just accept what was happening without doing anything? (v54) (*To fulfil the Old Testament which says it must happen this way.*)

PRAY

Remember this is all happening so that we can be rescued from our sin. Thank God.

Building up
Look at **Day 29** again. What did Jesus say the disciples would do? (*Scatter*) Read **Matthew 26v56** again. What did they do? (*Deserted Him.*) Isn't it good to know Jesus knows everything that will happen, and that He promises to always be with us.

DAY 32
On trial

Today's passages are:
Table Talk: Matthew 26v59-64
XTB: Matthew 26v57-68

TABLE TALK

A court is supposed to be a fair place. Who is in charge, to make sure the truth is told, and the right decision is made?

DO

Draw a picture of a Judge.
Let's see if Jesus gets a fair trial.

READ

Jesus was taken to Caiaphas the High Priest, where the teachers of the law and the elders had assembled.
Read Matthew 26v59-64

TALK

What were these leaders looking for? (v59) (*False evidence.*) What was their aim? (v59) (*To put Jesus to death.*) Finally, the religious leaders found some false witnesses. What final question did they ask Jesus? (v63) (*"Are you the Christ, the Son of God?"*) How did Jesus reply? (v64) (*"Yes I am."*)

Read verse 64 again. In the Old Testament, Daniel had a vision of a King who would judge the whole world and rule forever. (Daniel 7v13-14) In verse 64, Jesus says that's Him!

DO

Write "Jesus is Judge and Ruler of the world" under your picture of a judge.

PRAY

Praise God that Jesus is Judge and Ruler of the world!

Building up
Jesus was on trial and the religious leaders were trying to get false evidence against Him. If *you* were on trial, accused of being a follower of Jesus, what evidence could be given against you? Would there be enough to find you guilty?

DAY 33
Not me!

Today's passages are:
Table Talk: Matthew 26v69-75
XTB: Matthew 26v69-75

TABLE TALK

Recap: On Day 29 Peter said he wouldn't leave Jesus even if it meant dying. But how many times did Jesus say Peter would disown Him? (*Three*)

READ

After Jesus' arrest, Peter followed at a distance, to see what would happen.
Read Matthew 26v69-75

TALK

How did Peter deny Jesus each time? (v70—he denied it; v72—he denied it with an oath; v74—he called down curses and swore.) How was he reminded of what Jesus said He would do? (v74) (*A cock crowed.*) How did Peter react? (v75) (*He wept bitterly.*)

THINK

Peter was very upset when he realised he had let Jesus down. Have *you* let Jesus down? Talk about it together.

PRAY

We have all pretended not to know Jesus at some time. We need to say sorry and ask God to help us to tell people that Jesus is our friend.

Building up
Think about when you find it hardest to stand up for Jesus. What would help you in these situations? God promises to always be with you, to never leave you. Live with this promise in mind.

Notes for Parents
Three hours before the cross

Follow what happened to Jesus during these last few hours.

6.00am	Arrested. Taken to house of Caiaphas Sent to Pilate
7.00am	Sent to King Herod Returned to Pilate Barabbas freed, Jesus sentenced
8.30am	Led to Calvary
9.00am	Crucified

DAY 34
Guilty

KEYPOINT

Judas did wrong, knew it, but failed to ask for forgiveness.

Today's passages are:
Table Talk: Matthew 27v3-5
XTB: Matthew 27v1-10

TABLE TALK

Recap how Judas has been involved in the story so far.

READ

Early in the morning, the chief priests and the elders decided to put Jesus to death. So they handed Him over to Pilate. **Read Matthew 27v3-5**

TALK
Judas saw that Jesus had been condemned. Maybe things weren't as he had expected. How did he react? (v3) (*Seized with remorse and gave back the money he'd been paid.*)

Remorse means a strong feeling of regret and guilt for doing something wrong. What does Judas admit? (v4) (*"I have sinned."*)

Judas told the chief priests that Jesus was innocent. Did they care? (v4) (No!) They said it was *Judas'* problem, but really it was *their* problem too. Both Judas *and* the chief priests had turned their backs on Jesus.

THINK

They were both guilty and would be punished by God. Have you ever felt guilty about anything? The *only* way to forgiveness is to say sorry and ask God for forgiveness.

PRAY

Ask God to help you to realise when you need to say sorry to Him. Thank Him for sending Jesus as the way to forgiveness.

Building up
It is easy for us to think we are quite good and will be alright—but what does the Bible say? **Read 1 John 1:8-9** We must be honest with ourselves, honest with God, say sorry to Him and ask Him to forgive us.

DAY 35
Pilate's prisoners

KEYPOINT

Jesus is innocent, but is accused because the Chief Priests and Elders envy Him.

Today's passages are:
Table Talk: Matthew 27v11-19
XTB: Matthew 27v11-19

TABLE TALK
Have you been wrongly accused of doing something? What was it and how did you feel? (*If not, imagine how you would feel if someone accused you of stealing something from them.*)

READ

"It's not fair," might be a phrase you've said before. Jesus could have said that. **Read Matthew 27v11-19**

TALK

How did Jesus answer the chief priests? (v12&14) (*He said nothing.*) Jesus was **innocent** and Pilate knew that. How did he try to free Jesus? (v15-17) (*By using the custom of releasing a prisoner.*) Why did Pilate think the chief priests had handed Jesus over to him? (v18) (*Out of envy.*)

DO
On a piece of paper draw **Jesus** in prison. Write underneath, "Jesus, King of the Jews, Innocent". On the other side draw **Barabbas** in prison. Write "Barabbas, a rebel against the Romans, Guilty". *Keep your picture for tomorrow.*

PRAY

Tomorrow we will find out who Pilate released. But first! Praise Jesus that He never did anything wrong! Thank Him that He is the King of all the world.

Building up
Pilate asked Jesus, "Are you the King of the Jews?" (v11) Jesus said Yes. In fact, He is King of the whole world. Is He King of *your* life? How can you show this?

All about grace :
A PARENTS

Our culture has a habit of making Bible words mean something different from what they mean in the scriptures. So **Sin** becomes "something naughty but nice". **Faith** becomes believing something irrational and unprovable. And **Grace** becomes saying a prayer at meal times or looking elegant in a nice swishy dress!

What this means in terms of teaching our children is that we have to be extra careful to get things right, so that they will begin to understand what the Bible means by a word, and **over careful** to explain things, when the common usage of a word is different.

WHAT IS GRACE?

Grace is part of God's character: it describes how He acts towards us. Although we are sinners, and deserve God's judgement and punishment, nevertheless, He deals graciously with us by forgiving us through Jesus. In other words, Grace is God's undeserved favour towards us.

WHY IS IT IMPORTANT?

Understanding grace is very important, because it describes the whole way that God relates to us, and we to Him! Paul deliberately started and ended all of his letters by mentioning grace just to make this point. Unless we understand that God accepts us freely by His grace, through Jesus, then we will be doomed to thinking that we need to work to be better in order to make it into God's good books. This is the popular (and false!) view that many have of Christianity: be good and God will accept you into heaven. It actually works the opposite way round. "For by grace you have been saved through faith. And this is not your own doing; it is the gift of God, not a result of works, so that no one can boast" says Paul in Ephesians 2v8-9. So understanding grace is vital for becoming a Christian and being saved. It is also vital to understand it if we are to know how to go on in the Christian life. Because we are not only *saved* by grace, but we *live* by God's grace also.

Although all genuine Christians will grow in holiness and "work" for Christ in terms of acts of service, telling others etc., God's acceptance of us is not conditional on these things. We live in God's grace, knowing that, whatever happens, He is pleased with us, because of Christ. The downside of not understanding grace properly therefore is that we may either not be saved, or else we may try to live a Christian life based on doing things which will ultimately be joyless and enslaving.

TEACHING GRACE

It needs a bit of explaining, but the old mnemonic really does encapsulate the essence of what Grace is:

> *God's*
> *Riches*
> *At*
> *Christ's*
> *Expense*

In other words, God heaps upon us His love, forgiveness, acceptance into His family, heaven and all the other benefits of being His child when we don't deserve it. It is given to us not because we have earned it, but because Jesus bought it for us on the cross.

We might use human illustrations that are appropriate to them: "Supposing you had a friend who was being nasty and talking about you behind your back. You would be showing grace to them if you were friendly and offered to share a Kit Kat with them. [that is, you gave them something that they didn't deserve]."

THE WONDER OF GRACE

Grace is both odd and thrilling. Odd because it is not how we expect God to act—it seems a little daft. But thrilling because, if God has been gracious to us, then it is the equivalent of winning the lottery, without ever having bought a ticket! I'm forgiven, rich, going to live forever in heaven—and it has all come from Him. Understanding grace should make us truly thankful (which I guess is why they call saying thanks for food "grace").

LIVING GRACE

God not only offers to save us by Grace, but calls us to live by Grace too. That means that an essential part of showing your children the meaning of Grace is to model it in your own life. We must be forgiving and accepting of people, even when they don't deserve it. We pray for that every time we say the Lord's prayer: "forgive us our sins, even as we forgive others…"

And we must also try to model the wonder of knowing that, sinners and failures though we are, God is still pleased with us through Jesus. This could come across when we pray with our kids: "Lord, I really don't deserve your love, but thank you that you accept me…" In our conversations: "I'm amazed that God still loves me, even after I do such horrible things." Again, human illustrations can help here: "You may have trashed your room/written on the wall/disobeyed me (choose your own from a very long list), and I may be cross, upset or angry with you for that, but that will never change the fact that you are my child and that I love you, and will never turn you away."

Because of the nature of family life, most households need to work to a set of rules, and parents should expect their children to be obedient to their requests. But we must be careful that we do not start to model "works" in the way we live. We may be strict, but we also need to show that we are generous and forgiving. Parents who are too authoritarian have maybe forgotten how disobedient and difficult *we* were as children, and how gracious and forgiving our heavenly Father is, when we continue to live sinful lives.

ACTION PLAN

- Why not start by asking your children what they think the word "Grace" means.
- Try to explain it yourself, using some of the illustrations above, or ones of your own devising.
- Write out the mnemonic *God's Riches at Christ's Expense*, and put it somewhere prominent.
- Make sure that you remember to be thankful to God in your prayers—and honest about the fact that you don't deserve it.
- And please—to save the confusion—stop calling thanks for food "saying grace"…

Tim Thornborough
Saved by grace

> Grace is both odd and thrilling. Odd because it is not how we expect God to act—it seems a little daft. But thrilling because, if God has been gracious to us, then it is the equivalent of winning the lottery, without ever having bought a ticket!

BIBLE STORIES THAT ARE GOOD EXAMPLES OF GRACE:
Paul: Acts 9
The Siege of Samaria: 2 Kings 7
The penitent thief: Luke 23v32-43
The Unforgiving servant: Matt 18v21-35
Jesus forgiving Peter: John 21v15-17

DAY 36
Changing places

KEYPOINT
Jesus took Barabbas' place and punishment, and has done the same for us.

Today's passages are:
Table Talk: Matthew 27v20-26
XTB: Matthew 27v20-26

 TABLE TALK

Use yesterday's pictures to recap the story so far. Who are the two prisoners, who is guilty and who is innocent?

 READ

It was Pilate's custom to set a prisoner free. Who will it be?
Read Matthew 27v20-26

It was a very noisy place when Pilate asked the crowd who they wanted to be freed. Who did they say? (v20) (*Barabbas*) Who persuaded the crowd to choose him? (v20) (*The Jewish leaders.*)

So guilty Barabbas was freed, but innocent Jesus was held. What did the crowd want to happen to Him? (v22) (*"Crucify Him."*)

 THINK

The crowd, chief priests, elders and Pilate all ignored who Jesus was. The guilty were free, but the one man who was innocent was going to be punished. It's still **God's** plan though!

 DO

On the sheet from yesterday, write under **Barabbas**, "set free", and under **Jesus**, "sentenced to death on a cross".

 PRAY

We have seen rebels in our passage, but *we* are all guilty rebels too. We all deserve to be punished by God for ignoring Him and doing what we want. Thank Jesus for dying on the cross to take the punishment for your sins.

Building up
The ONLY way we can be put right with God, is through Jesus.
Read 1 Peter 3v18a (the first half of the verse)
Put this in your own words.

DAY 37
Mock honour

KEYPOINT
The soldiers didn't realise who Jesus was. They treated Him badly.

Today's passages are:
Table Talk: Matthew 27v27-31
XTB: Matthew 27v27-36

 TABLE TALK

When people claim something, which we find hard to believe, we sometimes make fun of them. Have you made fun of others? Talk about what happened.

 READ

Pilate handed Jesus over to his Roman soldiers. They were trained to be tough. This was not a fun situation for Jesus.
Read Matthew 27v27-31

 TALK

In a very short time Jesus had been marched from one part of Jerusalem to another. He had been questioned, accused and flogged. He was completely alone with a whole company of tough soldiers. What did they do to Him? (*Gave Him a scarlet robe, a crown of thorns, and a stick to carry. They pretended to honour Him as a king. Then they spat at Him, and hit Him.*) The soldiers knew what had gone on and didn't believe anything Jesus had claimed.

 THINK

Have you been made fun of? How did you feel?

Think again about what Jesus suffered for us! How do *you* treat Him—do you thank, praise and worship Him, or do you hurt and mock Him?

 PRAY

Ask God to help you treat Jesus in the right way.

Building up
Have you ever mocked others? Spend a few minutes thinking about people you know, who you have called names or given a hard time. How could you put right what you have done? Ask God to help you.

DAY 38
Prove it

KEYPOINT
The people, the Chief Priests and Elders all wanted Jesus to prove who He was.

Today's passages are:
Table Talk: Matthew 27v39-42
XTB: Matthew 27v37-44

TABLE TALK

Can you do anything amazing, like ride a bike, stand on your hands, play an instrument or something else? How would you feel if someone said they didn't believe you? How could you prove it? (*Prove some of them!—now or later.*)

READ

The people watching Jesus dying on the cross *don't believe* that He's God's Son. He *is* the Son of God—but He doesn't do anything to prove it!
Read Matthew 27v39-43

TALK

What did the **people** do and say? (v39-40) (*Hurled insults and told Him to save Himself by coming down from the cross.*) What did the **chief priests** do and say? (v41-42) (*Mocked Him and told Him to come down.*) But the chief priests and other leaders also turned on **God**. What did they say God should do? (v43) (*Rescue Him, because He said, "I am the Son of God".*)

THINK

If Jesus *had* come down from the cross, (and He could have done!), nobody would have been able to be saved. It is ONLY through Jesus we can be saved.

PRAY

Thank God that Jesus didn't save Himself, because He wanted to save us!

Building up
Read Matthew 27v32-38
What did the sign on Jesus' cross say? (v27) (*"This is Jesus, the King of the Jews."*) The sign was put there to mock Jesus—but it was true! Jesus is the King of Kings! Thank King Jesus for suffering on the cross to take the punishment for your sins.

DAY 39
Alone

KEYPOINT
For the first time ever, Jesus was completely alone, separated from God, just for us. It was terrible.

Today's passages are:
Table Talk: Matthew 27v45-46
XTB: Matthew 27v45-50

TABLE TALK

When I was a child, I remember feeling all alone. Think about some situations when you have felt all alone, or close your eyes and imagine it. Talk about it.

READ

Jesus had always been with God or been able to communicate with Him. But now things were different.
Read Matthew 27v45-46

TALK

Have you ever experienced it being dark during the day?

When was it dark in the passage? (v45) (*The 6th hour to 9th hour = 12 o'clock to 3 o'clock.*) Why do you think it went dark? (*As a sign of God's separation from Jesus; God's judgment.*)

THINK

Jesus hadn't done anything wrong. He is the only perfect person who has ever lived. So why did God punish Him by leaving Him completely alone? (*It was **our** sin, which God must punish, that caused **His** suffering; He took our punishment.*)

PRAY

Thank God that Jesus was separated from Him, so that you don't have to be.

Building up
Read Matthew 27v45-50 The people didn't understand what Jesus was doing. Do you understand how painful it was for Jesus, not just physically, but spiritually and emotionally? What's your reaction? Jesus loves you!

DAY 40
New openings

KEYPOINT
Jesus' death opened the way for sinners to be with God.

Today's passages are:
Table Talk: Matthew 27v50-52
XTB: Matthew 27v50-56

 TABLE TALK
Recap from Day 31. Was Jesus surprised by the things that happened to Him? (*No*) How do we know? (*He predicted it.*) Who was in control all the time? (*God was.*)

 READ
When Jesus died on the cross, strange things happened.
Read Matthew 27v50-52

 TALK
What strange events happened when Jesus died? (v51+52) (*Curtain was torn in two; earth shook and rocks split; tombs opened and dead Christians came to life.*)

 THINK
Jesus had opened the way for sinners to be with God. The temple curtain was a reminder that **sin** separated people from God! Jesus *destroyed* that separation, allowing everyone who believes to live forever with God!

 DO
On some paper, draw a cross in the middle, now draw four separate pictures around it: **1** Darkness; **2** A curtain torn down the middle; **3** Empty tombs; **4** Some guards with a speech bubble saying, "He is the Son of God" (v54)

 PRAY
Thank God for opening the way for sinners to live with Him for ever if they believe in Him.

Building up
Read Matthew 27v54-56 How did the Centurion and the others with him react? (*Terrified*) What did they say? ("*Surely He was the Son of God.*") How do *you* react to Jesus and what do you say about Him?

DAY 41
Definitely dead

KEYPOINT
Jesus was definitely dead. Joseph buried Jesus in his own new tomb.

Today's passages are:
Table Talk: Matthew 27v57-61
XTB: Matthew 27v57-61

 TABLE TALK

Yesterday we read of some strange events happening when Jesus died. What were they? (*See yesterday's list.*) In the next few readings, we see God's rescue plan unfolding some more.

 READ
Jesus is definitely dead!
Read Matthew 27v57-61

 TALK
Who went to Pilate and what did he ask? (v57+58) (*Joseph asked for Jesus' body.*) What did He do with Jesus' body? (v59+60) (*Wrapped it in a clean linen cloth and placed it in his new tomb.*)

Jesus' death had affected His followers. We know from Mark's Gospel that Joseph was a *secret* follower of Jesus. But after Jesus' death, he wanted to show his love for Jesus in *public*.

THINK
Do you show others your love for Jesus? How can you show your love for Him today?

 PRAY
Ask God for an opportunity to show people how much you love Jesus.

Building up
This story of Joseph is also told in John. Read **John 19v38-42** Who else is mentioned as a helper for Joseph? (*Nicodemus*) Also read **John 3v1-17** to find out about who Nicodemus was and see how he has changed.

DAY 42
Tomb raiders

 TABLE TALK

Look back at what Jesus predicted would happen in **Matthew 20v18-19** What did He say would happen?

 READ

So far everything has happened as Jesus said it would, but He is dead now. The Chief Priests and Pharisees don't need to worry anymore, do they?
Read Matthew 27v62-66

 TALK

What did the chief priests and Pharisees remember? (v63) (*That Jesus said He would rise again after three days.*) Do you think they believed Jesus would really come back to life? (*No!*) What did they want Pilate to do? (v64) (*Guard the tomb.*) What were they worried about? (v64) (*That the disciples would steal the body and claim that Jesus had risen.*)

 THINK

Even though He was dead, the chief priests and Pharisees were still worried about Jesus! How was the tomb made secure? (v65-66) (*A guard was posted and a seal was placed on the stone over the tomb.*)

PRAY

The chief priests and Pharisees wouldn't believe what Jesus said. Ask God to help *you* to believe all of Jesus' words.

Building up
Do you know people who won't accept that Jesus is who He says He is? What do they say about Him? Ask God to soften their hearts and reveal Himself to them.

DAY 43
Definitely alive!

 TABLE TALK

Play hangman to guess the word "resurrection" and/or look up *resurrection* in a dictionary.

 READ

The two Mary's had decided to go and look at the tomb where Jesus' body was. Things didn't turn out as they had expected. **Read Matthew 28v1-7**

 TALK

The scene that the two Mary's saw must have been very dramatic. What happened? (v2) (*Earthquake, and angel appeared and rolled the stone away and sat on it.*) What did the angel look like? (v3) (*Like lightning; his clothes were white as snow.*) Have you ever seen anything like that? Close your eyes and try to imagine it.

How did the guards react? (v4) (*Afraid, shook and became like dead men.*)

 THINK

Have you ever been scared and happy at the same time? This story is scary and happy. What did the angel say to the women? (v5-7) (*Don't be afraid, Jesus has risen, go tell the disciples.*)

 PRAY

Loving Jesus can sometimes mean we find ourselves in scary situations. But we can be happy too because He is still alive today! He is always there to help us. Ask Jesus to help you to tell others about Him, even when it can be scary.

Building up
Read Matthew 28v8-10 How did the women feel after meeting the angel? (v8) Who did they meet on the way? (v9) What was their reaction? (v9) Jesus told them to go and tell the others. So they did!

DAY 44
Spreading lies

KEYPOINT
Even though lies were spread, the truth is that **Jesus is Alive**.

Today's passages are:
Table Talk: Matthew 28v11-15
XTB: Matthew 28v11-15

 TABLE TALK

Telling lies can sometimes keep us from getting into trouble......for a while. But the truth always comes out eventually. *Have you told a lie and then been found out?* Talk about it and how you felt before and after being found out.

 READ

The chief priests are up to mischief again. **Read Matthew 28v11-15**

 TALK

The chief priests didn't like the news they received. What did they do? (v12-13) (*Devised a plan, accusing the disciples of stealing the body.*) Why did the soldiers agree to lie? (v12+15) (*They were given a large sum of money.*) This story is still going around today, and some people still believe the lie.

 THINK

How can we be sure to know the *truth*? **Look up 2 Timothy 3v16**
If we read God's Word, the Bible, regularly, we can be sure to know the truth and not be deceived by lies.

 PRAY

Dear God, help me to believe the truth that Jesus rose from the dead and is alive today.

Building up
Make the Easter Folding Square on the opposite page. Use it to remind yourselves of some of the key points of the Easter story. Now use it to explain the Easter story to someone else.

DAY 45
News for all

KEYPOINT
Jesus wants us to be His followers and tell others about Him. He promises to be with us.

Today's passages are:
Table Talk: Matthew 28v16-20
XTB: Matthew 28v16-20

 TABLE TALK

Although we hear and read about a lot of *bad* news, there is *good* news about too. What good news do you have to celebrate at the moment? When you have good news what do you do? (*Share it with others, celebrate.*)

 READ

Jesus is about to return to heaven, but He wants His followers to do something while He's gone. **Read Matthew 28v16-20**

 TALK

What does Jesus want His followers to make? (v19) (*Disciples/followers of all nations.*) What do His followers need to teach? (v20) (*Teach them to obey everything Jesus commanded.*) Why can He command His followers to do this? (v18) (*He has ALL authority, He's in charge of everything.*)

 THINK

This command from Jesus is for **us** too, but we can sometimes find this hard to do. Jesus makes a fantastic promise to help us. What is His promise? (v20) (*I am with you always.*)

> *"I will be with you always, to the end of the age."* Matthew 28v20

Copy this onto some paper, and put it where you'll all see it. Learn it together.

 PRAY

Pray for God's help to tell others about Him.

Building up
Read **Matthew 28v19-20** again. Jesus wants us to be His followers and tell others about Him. Have you ever told anyone about Him? Who could you tell about Jesus? Look and pray for the chance to tell them about Jesus. Remember "He is always with you".

DAY 44

Easter Folding Square

Make a fun reminder of some of the key points of the Easter story.

Instructions

1 Cut out the two main squares (sheets 1 & 2).

Sheet 1   Sheet 2

2 Fold along all dotted lines (into 16 smaller squares). *The model will work better with sharp creases.*

3 Stick the four corner squares (back) of Sheet 1 to the four corner squares (front) of Sheet 2.

4 Cut **down** the middle of Sheet 1. Cut **across** the middle of Sheet 2. (*This could be done before sticking.*)

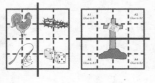

5 Try some folding and unfolding to see how different pictures come to the front. *Start by looking at Sheet 1, and folding it **out** from the middle.* Keep opening **out** the middle of each section until you're back to Sheet 1.

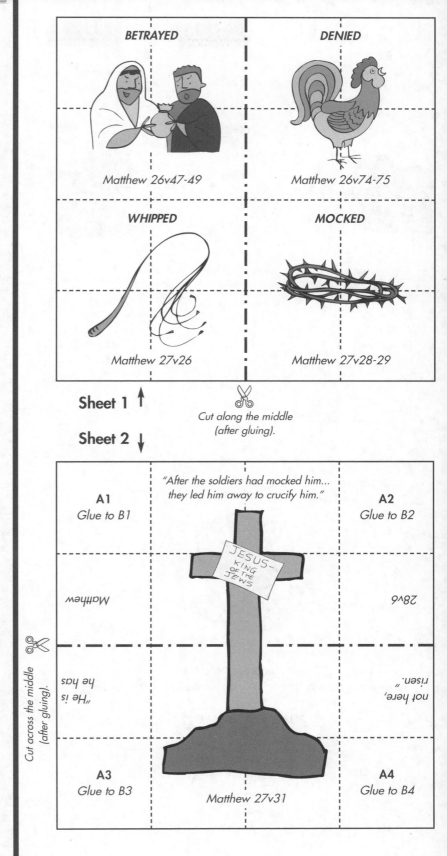

BETRAYED

Matthew 26v47-49

DENIED

Matthew 26v74-75

WHIPPED

Matthew 27v26

MOCKED

Matthew 27v28-29

Sheet 1 ↑

Cut along the middle (after gluing).

Sheet 2 ↓

Cut across the middle (after gluing).

A1
Glue to B1

"After the soldiers had mocked him... they led him away to crucify him."

A2
Glue to B2

Matthew

JESUS – KING OF THE JEWS

28v6

"He is he has

"not here, risen."

A3
Glue to B3

Matthew 27v31

A4
Glue to B4

"Truly this was the Son of God!"
Matthew 27v54

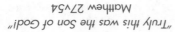

*"You will name him **Jesus**—because he will save his people from their sins."* Matthew 2v21

Do You Believe?

Easter Folding Square

See other side for instructions.

Notes for Parents

On eagle's wings

EXAMINING EXODUS
The book of Exodus shows us what God is like, and what God's people should be like...

What God is like

GOD IS THE KING
The first part of Exodus shows us that God is the true **King**. Nothing and no-one (not even Pharaoh, the powerful king of Egypt) can stop God's plans.

GOD IS THE RESCUER
God *rescued* the Israelites from Egypt, and continued to keep them safe as they travelled across the desert. As we saw on Days 16-25, He gave them food and water when needed, and rescued them from the Amalekites too.

What God's people should be like
The second half of Exodus shows us what God's rescued people should be like. They should:
- **Remember** what God has done.
- **Trust** God for the future.
- **Obey** God.

What about us?

If we are Christians, then *we* are God's rescued people too. As we have just been reading in Matthew, Jesus died and rose again to *rescue* us from our sin. As you read Exodus together, ask God to help you to *remember* what God has done for you, *trust* Him for the future and **obey** Him.

KEYPOINT
God is the Rescuing King. His people should remember what He's done, trust and obey Him.

Today's passages are:
Table Talk: Exodus 19v1-4
XTB: Exodus 19v1-4

TABLE TALK

*Note: Today's **Notes for Parents** outline some key themes in Exodus. You will find it helpful to read this beforehand. If you have older children, read it with them.*

Talk about how animals carry their young (eg: a cat carries a kitten in her mouth, a baby monkey clings to its mother's back, a kangaroo has a pouch...)

READ

In today's reading, God has a message for the Israelites. He uses the picture of a mother eagle and her young. **Read Exodus 19v1-4**

TALK

The Israelites had been travelling in the desert for three months. Where did they stop? (v2) (*At the foot of Mount Sinai.*) God had a message for the Israelites (called the house of Jacob). What did God say He was like? (v4) (*An eagle carrying her young on her wings.*)

THINK

Like an eagle cares for her young, God had powerfully rescued the Israelites from danger and brought them to be with Him. Read "What God's people should be like" in **Notes for Parents**. This is what the Israelites should be like—and what *we* should be like too.

PRAY

As you read Exodus together, ask God to help you to be like this.

Building up
If you haven't yet done so, read through **Notes for Parents** together. Look up **Exodus 14v30-31** to see how the Israelites responded when God brought them through the Red Sea. In the next few days we'll see if they'll *continue* to trust God and Moses.

God's chosen people

Ready for God

KEYPOINT
The Israelites are God's chosen people. They are to obey Him.

Today's passages are:
Table Talk: Exodus 19v5 & 8
XTB: Exodus 19v5-8

KEYPOINT
God is awesome. Nothing impure can come near Him.

Today's passages are:
Table Talk: Exodus 19v9-11
XTB: Exodus 19v9-13

TABLE TALK

Imagine having a treasure chest. What would you each keep in it?

DO

Draw a picture of a treasure chest. Write these words on it: "If you obey me fully and keep my covenant, then you will be my treasured possession." (Ex 19v5)

READ

This is God's message for the Israelites. **Read Exodus 19v5**

TALK

The **covenant** is an agreement between God and His people. What does God say His special treasure is? (v5) (*The Israelites. They are God's chosen people.*) What does God say they are to do? (*Obey Him.*)

Read **Exodus 19v8** to see how the Israelites reply. How much of God's word do they say they'll obey? (v8) (*Everything*)

THINK

The Israelites have said that they will obey God in *everything*. But as we'll see in Exodus, they aren't able to do so. They will fail God many times.

PRAY

Living God's way is hard. Like the Israelites, we will often let Him down. (*We all sin. That's why Jesus died for us as our Rescuer.*) Say sorry to God for letting Him down. Ask Him to help you to live His way.

TABLE TALK

Imagine that the Queen is coming to visit. How would you get ready? (*eg: clean the house, put on best clothes...*)

READ

The Israelites also needed to get ready— to meet with **God**.
Read Exodus 19v9-11

TALK

Where would the people hear God speaking from? (v9) (*A thick cloud.*) The people were to *purify* (or *consecrate*) themselves, so that they were ready for God. How were they to do that? (v10) (*Wash their clothes.*) This wasn't because they were muddy! They washed their clothes to be ready to meet with God.

THINK

God is amazing, powerful and perfect. He is totally pure, and nothing impure can come near Him! He was going to put on a display of His awesome power—but the Israelites mustn't come too close. So God told Moses to set limits to stop people going up the mountain. (v12-13)

PRAY

God is still awesome today. We have no right to be near Him. He is too perfect. Too pure. But the great news is that we *can* come to God because of Jesus! Thank God that Jesus died to make a way for us to be with Him.

Building up

Read Exodus 19v5-8 God told the Israelites they were to be a "kingdom of priests and a holy nation". **Priests** served God and told others about Him. The Israelites were to do this too. **Holy** means "set apart". They were set apart to be *different* from the other nations, because they belonged to God. Today, *Christians* are God's chosen people. We too are to serve Him and tell others about Him.

Building up

Read Exodus 19v12-13 The limits protected the people from going up the mountain and being killed. But they would also be a picture, reminding the people that nothing impure could come near God. Do you sometimes forget how awesome and pure God is? Praise Him now, and ask Him to help you to understand more about what He is really like.

Thunder struck

KEYPOINT
God gave the Israelites a glimpse of His awesome power.

Today's passages are:
Table Talk: Exodus 19v16-19
XTB: Exodus 19v16-25

DO

(*You need paper and pencil.*)
Draw Mount Sinai.

Yesterday, we saw that Moses was to set *limits* to stop people going up the mountain.
Draw a line at the bottom of the mountain, to show where they must stop.

READ

Today, it's time for the people to see for themselves how awesome God is.
Read Exodus 19v16-19

TALK

What did the people hear? (v16) (*Thunder and a loud trumpet blast.*)
What did they see? (*v16—a thick cloud; v18—smoke and fire.*)

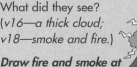

DO

Draw fire and smoke at the top of the mountain.

How did the people feel? (v16) (*They trembled with fear.*)

Wow! The Israelites would never forget this day! It would remind them of how **awesome** God is.

PRAY

Think of some words to describe God. (*eg: loving, powerful...*) Write them round your picture. Thank and praise God that He is like this.

Building up
Read Exodus 19v20-25 Moses had already set limits to stop the people going up the mountain. Why do you think God wanted Moses to warn them again? (*We're not told, but maybe their curiosity would have got the better of them. God didn't want anyone to be hurt.*)

The ten commandments

KEYPOINT
God's rescued people must put **God** first in their lives.

Today's passages are:
Table Talk: Exodus 20v1-6
XTB: Exodus 20v1-6

TABLE TALK

Recap: On Day 46 we saw what God's rescued people are to be like. (*If you want a reminder, it's in Notes for Parents, Day 46.*) What are they to **remember**? (*What God has done for them.*) Who are they to **trust**? (*God*) Who are they to **obey**? (*God*)

READ

At Mt Sinai, God gave the Israelites some commandments, to show them how to live. Do you know how many there were? (*Ten*) We're going to read about the first two today. **Read Exodus 20v1-6**

TALK

What does God remind the Israelites? (v2) (*He's their God, who rescued them from Egypt.*) What two rules does He give them? (v3+4) (*v3—No other gods; v4—No idols.*)

THINK

An *idol* is anything we worship instead of God. In Bible times, people often made statues to pray to. But an idol today can be anything we treat as being more important than God.

PRAY

What kind of things might *you* be tempted to put first, instead of God? (*eg: family, sport, friends, money...*) We *all* break these two commandments! None of us always puts God first. Tell God you're sorry for making other things more important than Him. Ask Him to help you to love *Him* more than anything else.

Building up
Some things have changed since the time of Exodus. (We are unlikely to make statues to pray to!) But God does *not* change! His character is the same as we see in Exodus. And the principles behind the ten commandments still apply today. They help us to see how to live as God's rescued people—to please Him.

DAY 51
What's in a name?

Today's passages are:
Table Talk: Exodus 20v7
XTB: Exodus 20v7

TABLE TALK

Draw a crown on some paper. Write "Rescuing King" under it. What have we read in Exodus that shows that God is the Rescuing King? (*eg: God **rescued** the Israelites from Egypt. He showed that He is the **true King** of the world, unlike Pharaoh who thought he was the most powerful king around.*)

READ

God is awesome, powerful and perfect. Even His *name* is special! The third commandment showed the Israelites how they should treat their Rescuing King. **Read Exodus 20v7**

TALK

What were they told *not* to do? (*Not to misuse God's name.*) Can you think of some examples? (*eg: don't use God's name [or "Jesus"] as a swear word; never joke about God; don't think wrong things about God.*)

THINK

Imagine what it would be like if someone used *your* name as a swear word! How would it make you feel?
God always hears us if we say or think wrong things about Him. Imagine how it makes Him feel.

PRAY

If you ever use God's name as a swear word, or think wrong things about Him, tell Him you are sorry. Ask Him to help you to change.

Building up
Look back to **Exodus 3v14-15**, where God first told Moses His name. What does this name tell us about God? (*God never changes. He is everlasting. He is always with us.*)

DAY 52
Rest is best

Today's passages are:
Table Talk: Exodus 20v8-11
XTB: Exodus 20v8-11

TABLE TALK

Note: *Please read **Notes for Parents** (opposite) about the Sabbath.*

Which days do you go to school/work? Imagine never getting a day off! How would you feel?

READ

The fourth commandment is about having a rest. **Read Exodus 20v8-11**

TALK

God made our world, and then rested. (v11) This was the pattern for the Israelites too. How many days were they to work for? (v9) (*Six*) What were they to do on the seventh day (the Sabbath)? (v10) (*Rest*)

THINK

A day of rest doesn't mean spending all day sleeping! It's a great day to meet with other Christians to learn together about Jesus. It's also a great day to do something you enjoy. What are some of the things you enjoy doing (together, as well as on your own), that you could do on your rest day?

Note: *For many of us, our rest day is Sunday—but it doesn't have to be. The most important thing is building rest into our weekly schedule.*

PRAY

Ask God to help you to make one day special.

Building up
On Days 19-21 we read about God giving the Israelites *manna* to eat. They had to collect it each morning. Can you remember what happened on the Sabbath? Check your answer in **Exodus 16v23-26**. God made sure they had enough food for every day without having to work on the Sabbath!

DAY 52 & 55
Notes for Parents

THE SABBATH (Day 52)

This can be a tricky topic. Children sometimes have very little say in what they do each day, which can make it hard for them to choose to make one day special. Think about how you can help them to take some responsibility in making their rest day special.

Also, be ready to talk honestly about your own patterns of work. Do your working hours mean that your children rarely see you? Do you take your day of rest?

Does your pattern of family life give you a day each week when you can do things you enjoy together? If not, what can you change?

FAITHFUL RELATIONSHIPS (Day 55)

The seventh commandment (Do not commit adultery) may raise some difficult issues for you or your children. It may be that you have experienced the pain of a marriage break-up. Certainly, your children will know others who have. Reassure your child that God **loves** them, and each member of their family. Reassure them that *you* love them too. Encourage them to pray about any worries they have, and maybe to talk them through with an older Christian.

God is always **faithful**—and *our* faithfulness matters to Him too. For those of us who are married, God says we are to be faithful to our marriage partner. And that we must not break up someone else's marriage. But we are to be faithful in our other relationships too. That includes fidelity in our *friendships*—not turning our backs on our friends, letting them down or gossiping about them. This applies to children and adults alike. Our relationships should mirror the faithfulness of our God.

DAY 53
Mums and Dads

KEYPOINT
We are to honour our parents. This pleases God.

Today's passages are:
Table Talk: Exodus 20v12
XTB: Exodus 20v12

TABLE TALK

Take turns to see who can do the most flourishing curtsy or bow.

READ

The fifth commandment is about "honouring" your parents. Does this mean bowing to them? Let's find out. **Read Exodus 20v12**

TALK

What does this law say we should do? (*Honour/respect our parents.*)

This doesn't mean bowing to them! Think carefully about how you react when your parents ask you to do something. Do you complain? Put it off? Do it straight away?

There's a really good reason for obeying straight away. Look up **Colossians 3v20**. What reason does this verse give? (*It pleases God.*)

THINK

Think of some ways that you can *please God* by honouring your parents. (eg: Do what they say without grumbling; Thank them for taking care of you; Help at home without being asked.) (*Adults—can you apply this to your own parents, too?*)

PRAY

Each choose one of these ideas that you will do today. Ask God to help you.

Building up

Spend some time praying for each other.

Children: Being a good parent isn't easy! Ask God to help your parents to be good parents.

Parents: Being obedient isn't easy either! Ask God to help your children to respect you, and to obey you without grumbling.

DAY 54
Murder mystery

KEYPOINT
God made and loves each person. It's wrong to murder them—or to hate, fight or insult them.

Today's passages are:
Table Talk: Ex 20v13 & Matthew 5v21-22
XTB: Matthew 5v21-22

TABLE TALK

Recap: Can you remember the first five commandments? (*1—No other gods; 2—No idols; 3—Don't misuse God's name; 4—Keep one day special; 5—Honour your parents.*)

The sixth commandment is very short.
Read Exodus 20v13

> *God made and loves* everyone in the world. He chose to give each person life. *So it's wrong* to take their life away by murdering them.

But Jesus said this commandment is about *more* than murder.
Read Matthew 5v21-22

TALK

Who did Jesus say this commandment is about? (v22) (*Anyone who is angry with "his brother"—which means everyone, not just your little brother!*)

> *God made and loves* each person. *So it's wrong* to hate them, fight with them, or call them names.

DO

Draw a large heart. Inside it, write:
"God is a God of love.
So <u>we</u> should be
loving too."

PRAY

See *Building Up* (below) for ideas on how to pray together.

Building up

Is there anyone you find it really hard to like? Do you ever tease people? Or ignore them? (*Adults, you need to be honest here too.*) Pray together about your answers. Ask God to help you to change, and to treat people the way **He** wants you to.

DAY 55
Family matters

KEYPOINT
Our faithfulness in relationships should mirror God's. We should be faithful in marriage.

Today's passages are:
Table Talk: Exodus 20v14
XTB: Exodus 20v14

TABLE TALK

Note: *Please read **Notes for Parents** (on the previous page) about Faithful Relationships.*

Play hangman to guess "marriage" *and/or* look it up in a dictionary.

READ

Read Exodus 20v14

1—God invented marriage. He said that marriage should be for life. So this seventh commandment says that you mustn't take someone else's husband or wife (adultery).

2—Families matter to God. This command protects families from being broken up.

TALK

Who are the people in *your* family? (*If you can, draw quick pictures of them, or write their names in a family tree.*)

PRAY

Thank God for each person in your family. Then choose *two* of these ways to pray:

• Is anyone in your family sad, worried or ill? Ask God to help them.

• Have you done anything special together as a family, or are you planning to? Thank God for special times together.

• Is there anything about your family that makes you sad? Talk to God about it.

• Ask God to help you to love each person in your family, and to find ways to show them that you love them.

Building up

As with yesterday's commandment, Jesus developed this command in the Sermon on the Mount. With older children it may be appropriate to read **Matthew 5v27-28**. Help them to see that what they *think* and *say* about people can be just as wrong as what they *do*.

DAY 56
Do not steal

KEYPOINT
If we steal, it shows that we don't trust God and don't love people the way God wants.

Today's passages are:
Table Talk: Exodus 20v15
XTB: Exodus 20v15

TABLE TALK

Note: If your child is nervous about burglars in the night, skip this first bit. Have you ever been burgled, or know someone who has? How did it make you/them feel?

READ

We've reached commandment number eight. **Read Exodus 20v15**

THINK

The Bible tells us that **God** gives us everything we have, and that He gives us *good* gifts. *But if we steal* extra things for ourselves, what does that show? (*We don't trust God to give us everything we need.*)

The Bible tells us that God made and loves everyone—and that we should love them too. *But if we steal* from people, what does that show? (*We don't love them the way God wants.*)

TALK

Stealing is more than just breaking into houses. Talk (honestly!) about the following: Have you ever shoplifted? Borrowed something and not returned it? Taken stuff you weren't supposed to? Dodged a bus fare?

PRAY

If you have ever stolen anything, say sorry to God. Ask Him to help you to change—and to trust *Him* for everything you need.

Building up
In Ephesians 4, Paul is developing the idea that as Christians we put off our old (sinful) nature and put on our new nature. Read **Ephesians 4v28**. What should the thief do instead of stealing? (*Honest work.*) Why? (*To have enough to share with others.*) Do *you* share what you have with others?

DAY 57
Lie hearted

KEYPOINT
God's people should only speak the truth—just as God does.

Today's passages are:
Table Talk: Exodus 20v16
XTB: Exodus 20v16

TABLE TALK

Read or act out this story:
Sam: I hate Joe! Let's get him into trouble.
Phil: OK. We'll tell Mr Green that Joe nicked your new trainers.
Sam: Yeah, great! That'll sort him!

READ

The ninth commandment is about this.
Read Exodus 20v16

TALK

Giving "false testimony" means lying about someone. In the story, why were Sam and Phil wrong? (*They were breaking God's ninth commandment. Joe would be punished for something he hadn't done.*)

THINK

God is **totally loving**, and His words are **always true**. So what should God's people be like? (*Only speaking the truth—just as God does; Loving each other—just as God loves them.*) Sam and Phil were wrong for *these* reasons too,

If we are Christians (God's people), we should be like God and show others what He is like. God is loving and truthful. We should be too.

PRAY

Say **sorry** to God for any times you have lied about someone else. **Thank** God that His words are always true. Ask Him to help you to be truthful too.

Building up
The witnesses at Jesus' trial were breaking this commandment. **Read Matthew 26v59-61** What they did was wrong—but **God** was always in control. He used their lies, and the envy of the Jewish leaders, for His *own* good purposes!

DAY 58
It's not fair!

 TABLE TALK

Each think of something that a friend has, that *you* would like to have too. What is it and why would you like it?

 READ

The last commandment is about *coveting*, which means longing to have something that someone else has.
Read Exodus 20v17

 TALK

What were the Israelites told *not* to covet (desire)? (*See list in v17.*) If you're like me, you've probably never wanted someone else's ox! But what kind of things might *you* get jealous about? (*Someone else's bike, computer, clothes, car, puppy…?*)

 THINK

 Two days ago we saw that if we **steal**, it shows that we don't *trust* God to give us everything we need. **Coveting** is similar. If we are jealous of what other people have, what are we saying about God? (*That He hasn't given us enough, and that we want more.*)

PRAY

Have you ever coveted something that wasn't yours? Clothes? Friends? Money? If you have, say sorry to God and ask Him to help you not to get jealous. Ask God to help you to trust Him to give you everything you need.

Building up
Think of the many things God has given you. (*Possessions, family, a home, friends…*) Ask God to help you to remember that everything you have is a gift from Him. Thank God for all that He has given you.

DAY 59
The greatest command

1 No other gods	6 Do not murder
2 No idols	7 Don't commit adultery
3 Don't misuse God's name	8 Do not steal
4 Keep one day special	9 Don't lie about others
5 Honour your parents	10 Don't be jealous of others

Think back over all ten commandments. Which do you think is the most important, and why?

 READ

Some of Jesus' enemies (religious leaders called Pharisees and Sadducees) asked Jesus the same question.
Read Matthew 22v34-40

 TALK

Jesus gave two commands (both of which come from the Old Testament). What was the first? (*See v37.*) This means loving God *totally*, with every part of you.

What was the second command? (*See v39.*) This means loving *everyone*, not just neighbours!

In v40, Jesus says these two commands sum up all of God's law.

 THINK

(*Optional*) Look again at the ten commandments. Which ones are about **loving God**? Which ones are about **loving other people**?

PRAY

Jesus' words mean that we must love God totally, and love other people just as much as we love ourselves. That's really hard to do! So ask God to help you.

Building up
The two commands Jesus gives are from the Old T. Look them up in **Deuteronomy 6v4-5** and **Leviticus 19v18**. Copy Jesus' two commands onto some paper. Put it somewhere you'll all see it often. Learn these words as your next **Memory Verse**.

DAY 60
We will...

Today's passages are:
Table Talk: Exodus 24v3 & 8
XTB: Exodus 24v3-8

TABLE TALK

As well as the ten commandments, God gave Moses many other instructions about how the Israelites were to live. (*They're in chapters 20-23.*) How do you think they'll respond? *a)* "We're not going to bother with your laws." *b)* "They sound hard, but we'll give it a go." *c)* "We'll do everything you say."

READ

Read Exodus 24v3

What did the Israelites say? (*"We'll do everything the Lord has said."*)

In the morning, Moses built an altar—a stone table where they cooked special animals and gave them as a sacrifice (gift) to God. Then Moses took some of the blood from the sacrifices, and sprinkled it on the people.
Read Exodus 24v8

THINK

A **covenant** is a special agreement that mustn't be broken. God *always* kept His part of the covenant. He took care of the Israelites and kept all of His promises to them.

What h-u-g-e promise had the Israelites just made to God? (*To obey **everything** He said.*) Do you think they'll keep their promise? (*We'll find out tomorrow...*)

PRAY

God **never** makes promises that He can't keep! Thank Him for being like this.

Building up
This covenant between God and His people was sealed with blood. Does that remind you of anything Jesus said? **Read Matthew 26v26-28** This **new** covenant is the way for us to have our sins forgiven and be right with God. Thank Jesus for dying for you so that your sins could be forgiven.

DAY 61
Calf hearted

Today's passages are:
Table Talk: Exodus 32v1-4
XTB: Exodus 32v1-6

TABLE TALK

What huge promise have the Israelites just made to God? (*To obey everything He said.*) Read the cartoon story in **Notes for Parents** (on the next page) to find out what happened next.

READ

Read Exodus 32v1-4

Moses was on Mount Sinai for 40 days and nights (Exodus 24v18). Meanwhile, what did the Israelites tell Aaron to do? (v1) (*Make gods for them.*) What did Aaron collect from the people? (v2) (*Their gold earrings.*) What did he make? (v4) (*A statue of a calf.*) What did the Israelites say about the statue? (v4) (*That it was their god, who rescued them from Egypt.*)

TALK

Why is this shocking? (*They've broken their promise, and seem to have forgotten all that God has done for them.*)

As we read Exodus, we often see the Israelites forget what God has done for them, and stop trusting Him. Sadly, **we** are like this too. All of us easily forget God and turn away from Him.

THINK

Say sorry to God for the times when you have turned away from Him. Ask Him to help you never to forget what He's done for you, and to keep trusting Him, no matter how hard that is.

PRAY

Building up
Which of the ten commandments are the Israelites breaking here? Check your answer in **Exodus 20v1-6**.

THE GOLDEN CALF

The Israelites had just promised to obey all God's laws. But while Moses was up Mount Sinai, they got restless...

Moses was on Mount Sinai with God. He was there for 40 days and nights.

So the Israelites went to Aaron, Moses' brother.

We don't know what's happened to Moses.

Make gods for us, to lead us.

Aaron agreed.

Bring me all your gold earrings

So the people brought their earrings to Aaron.

And Aaron made them into a statue of a golden calf.

The people worshipped the statue.

These are our gods, who led us out of Egypt!

Then they held a festival to celebrate.

DAY 62
Stiff-necked people

> **KEYPOINT**
> The Israelites were stiff-necked, turning away from God. But God was merciful to them.

Today's passages are:
Table Talk: Exodus 32v11-14
XTB: Exodus 32v7-14

TABLE TALK

Have you ever tried to make a dog (or donkey!) go somewhere it doesn't want to go? What does it do?

READ

The Israelites were like this! God had shown them the *best way* to live. But like stubborn donkeys they refused, and went their *own way* instead, making a golden calf to worship. So God called them **stiff-necked!** A stubborn people. He was very angry and threatened to destroy them. But Moses pleaded with God.
Read Exodus 32v11-14

TALK

If God destroyed the Israelites, what would the Egyptians say? (v12) (*That God only rescued them so that He could kill them later.*) The Israelites were the family of Abraham, Isaac and Jacob. What had God promised them? (v13) (*A huge family and a land of their own.*) There already were huge numbers of Israelites (2-3 million), but they hadn't yet reached the promised land of Canaan.

THINK

Did God destroy the Israelites? (v14) (*No*) The Israelites had **sinned**. They *deserved* to die. But instead God showed them **mercy**—*undeserved* kindness. (*We'll find out more about sin, anger and mercy tomorrow.*)

PRAY

Thank God that He is **merciful**—showing loving kindness to all His people (including you and me!) when we don't deserve it.

Building up
Read the first part of the story for yourself in
Exodus 32v7-10.

Anger and mercy

Notes for Parents

KEYPOINT
Sin must always be punished, but God shows us great mercy (in particular by sending Jesus).

Today's passages are:
Table Talk: Exodus 32v19-20
XTB: Exodus 32v15-20

TABLE TALK

READ

TALK

THINK

DO

PRAY

Recap: Ask your child to tell you the story of the Golden Calf in their own words, *or* re-read the cartoon version opposite.

Yesterday we saw that God was **angry** with the Israelites. When Moses came down from the mountain, and saw the golden calf, *he* was angry too.
Read Exodus 32v19-20

Moses was carrying two stone tablets with the ten commandments written on them. What did he do with them? (v19) (*Break them.*) What did Moses do with the golden calf? (*See v20*)

The Israelites had **sinned**. And sin must always be punished. Some of them died because of what they had done, and others became ill. (This is in v25-35.) *God could not let their sin go unpunished.*

That's true for *us* too. We all sin—and sin *must* be punished. But the great news is that someone came to take the punishment in our place! Who? (*Jesus*)

Use the *Book illustration* (*see Notes for Parents on the right*) to show how Jesus took the punishment we deserve.

Sin must always be punished. But God showed us great **mercy** (undeserved kindness) by sending Jesus to die in our place. Thank God for this!

Building up

Read some other verses about God's great mercy: **Romans 12v1-2, Titus 3v4-5a, 1 Peter 2v9-10** Thank and praise God for His mercy towards you.

THE BOOK ILLUSTRATION

This is a simple and effective way of explaining how Jesus died to rescue us. Use any book (*except a Bible, because the book stands for our sin!*)

Hold up your right hand. Explain that your hand represents you, and that the ceiling stands for God. Show the book, and ask them to imagine that it contains a record of your sin—every time you have done, said or thought things that are wrong. Put the book flat on your right hand.

Ask: "What does the book do?"
It separates you from God. This is a picture of what sin does. It gets in the way between us and God, and stops us knowing Him as our Friend.

Now hold up your left hand. This stands for Jesus. Explain that Jesus lived a perfect life. He never sinned. There was nothing separating Jesus from God.

Explain that as Jesus died on the cross, the sin of the whole world was put onto Him. Transfer the book from your right hand to your left hand to show this.

Ask: "What is there between Jesus and God?"
This is why Jesus died—to take the punishment for all our sin.

Now look back at your right hand.
Ask: "What is there between me and God?"
The answer is—Nothing!

When Jesus died on the cross, He took the punishment for our sins so that we can be forgiven. This means that there is **nothing** to separate us from God any more. This was **God's Rescue Plan** for us.

DAY 64
Still stiff-necked

KEYPOINT
The Israelites are still stiff-necked, but God makes them amazing promises.

Today's passages are:
Table Talk : Exodus 33v1-3 & 15-17
XTB : Exodus 33v1-17

TABLE TALK

Try being "stiff-necked" for a minute. eg: try nodding, bowing, touching your toes etc. *without* moving your neck!

READ

When the Israelites turned away from God and worshipped a golden calf instead, He called them **stiff-necked** (meaning stubborn). They are *still* a stiff-necked, stubborn people, who will turn away from God again. But now God gives them a *promise*...
Read Exodus 33v1-3

TALK

What promise is God keeping? (v1) (*To give them a land of their own, Canaan.*) Who will God send with them? (v2) (*An angel.*) But who will *not* go with them? (v3) (*God!*) Why? (*Because He might destroy them on the way.*)

READ

But Moses knew that they *needed* God to go with them. In a special meeting tent, He pleaded with God...
Read Exodus 33v15-17

TALK

If God wouldn't go with them, what did Moses want? (v15) (*That they stay where they are—in the desert.*) Did God agree to go with them? (v17) (*Yes*)

PRAY

The Israelites were still stubborn sinners. They didn't *deserve* to be given the promised land, or to have God go with them. But God gave them these amazing promises—because He's so loving and merciful. Thank God for being like this.

Building up
Like the Israelites, *we* are still stiff-necked. We are stubborn sinners. But God keeps His promises to us too—because He's so loving and merciful. Praise and thank Him!

DAY 65
God's glory

KEYPOINT
God is good. He shows mercy and compassion.

Today's passages are:
Table Talk : Exodus 33v18-23
XTB : Exodus 33v18-23

TABLE TALK

Give your child clues (words or pics) to guess some of the amazing things **Moses** has seen. (*eg: burning bush, plagues, manna, smoke and fire on Mt Sinai...*)

READ

Now Moses asks to see one more thing. **Read Exodus 33v18-23**

TALK

What did God warn Moses he *couldn't* see? (v20) (*God's face.*) But what *would* Moses see? (v23) (*God's back.*) Moses would *see* just a *little* of what God is like.

But he also **heard** what God is like. What did Moses hear? (v19) (*God's name. That God shows mercy and compassion.*) As we saw on Day 62, **mercy** means showing incredible kindness to someone who doesn't deserve it. **Compassion** is caring for people in trouble.

The rest of Exodus shows how God continued to show *mercy* and *compassion* to the Israelites. Even when they sinned against Him, God kept *all* of His promises to them.

THINK

Are *you* like Moses? Do you want to know God better and discover more about Him? Like Moses, we can't see God's face yet. Not until we live with Him for ever in heaven! But we *can* get to know God better, by reading His book, the Bible.

PRAY

Ask God to help you keep getting to know Him better as you read the Bible together.

Building up
Read **Psalm 103**. (*All of it if you have time, otherwise v6-14.*) This great poem shows us what God is like. Which of these characteristics have you seen while reading Exodus together?

Extra Readings

WHY ARE THERE EXTRA READINGS?

Table Talk and **XTB** both come out every three months. The main Bible reading pages contain material for 65 days. That's enough to use them Monday to Friday for three months.

Many families find that their routine is different at weekends from during the week. Some find that regular Bible reading fits in well on school days, but not at weekends. Others encourage their children to read the Bible for themselves during the week, then explore the Bible together as a family at weekends, when there's more time to do the activities together.

The important thing is to help your children get into the habit of reading for the Bible for themselves—and that they see that regular

Bible reading is important for **you** as well.

If you **are** able to read the Bible with your children every day, that's great! The extra readings on the next page will augment the main **Table Talk** pages so that you have enough material to cover the full three months.

You could:

- Read **Table Talk** every day for 65 days, then use the extra readings for the rest of the third month.

- Read **Table Talk** on weekdays. Use the extra readings at weekends.

- Use any other combination that works for your family.

TIME TO REMEMBER...

Hopefully you have learned four memory verses as you've read this issue of XTB. These extra readings would all make great memory verses too. They're all about **Jesus**—about why He came, and how we can follow Him. Choose one or two to learn as you read them.

There are 26 Bible readings on the next three pages. Part of each verse has been printed for you—but with a word missing. Fill in the missing words as you read the verses. Then see if you can find them all in the wordsearch.

Note: Some are written backwards—or diagonally!!

F	A	T	H	E	R	E	S	H	E	P	H	E	R	D
I	R	H	E	W	A	Y	W	A	Y	O	U	T	E	O
N	S	I	R	E	I	G	O	O	D	O	K	O	T	G
V	A	S	E	N	S	E	R	P	R	A	Y	D	U	E
I	V	E	S	N	E	E	D	E	E	R	O	A	R	R
S	I	V	A	N	D	T	A	B	L	E	Y	Y	N	U
I	O	O	Y	O	U	S	L	U	F	K	N	A	H	T
B	U	L	O	S	T	T	A	L	K	J	X	T	B	P
L	R	E	J	O	I	C	E	L	O	K	E	Y	Y	I
E	X	T	B	R	A	C	E	A	B	L	E	S	O	R
D	E	A	T	H	C	A	L	M	S	A	F	E	U	C
B	E	L	I	E	V	E	S	B	T	I	R	I	P	S

Extra Readings

Memory Verses about Jesus

1 ☐ **Read Hebrews 13v8**

*Jesus **never** changes. Everything we read about Him in these extra readings will be true for **ever**.*

"Jesus Christ is the same yesterday,

t _ _ _ _ and forever." (v8)

2 ☐ **Read John 14v6**

*Jesus is the **only** way to know God.*

Jesus said, "I am the

w _ _ , the truth and the life; no one goes to the Father except by me." (v6)

3 ☐ **Read John 1v29**

Jesus died to take the punishment for our sin.

"There is the **L** _ _ _ of God, who takes away the sin of the world!" (v29)

4 ☐ **Read Acts 2v24**

Jesus rose again from the dead. He is still alive today!

"But God raised Him from **d** _ _ _ _ _ setting Him free from its power, because it was impossible that death should hold Him prisoner." (v24)

5 ☐ **Read John 10v14-15**

Jesus described Himself as our <u>good</u> shepherd, who dies for His sheep.

"I am the good **S** _ _ _ _ _ _ _ ."
(v14)

Memory Verses about why Jesus came

6 ☐ **Read Colossians 1v15**

Jesus shows us what God is like.

"Christ is the visible likeness of the

i _ _ _ _ _ _ _ _ God. He is the firstborn over all creation." (v15)

7 ☐ **Read Matthew 1v21**

An angel told Joseph that Jesus was coming to save us.

"She will have a son, and you will name him **J** _ _ _ _ —because he will save his people from their sins." (v21)

8 ☐ **Read Luke 2v11-14**

The angels told the shepherds that Jesus, their Rescuer, had been born.

"This very day in David's town your

S _ _ _ _ _ _ _ was born—Christ the Lord!" (v11)

9 ☐ **Read John 3v16**

The most famous verse in the Bible!

"For God loved the world so much that He gave His only Son, so that everyone who

b _ _ _ _ _ _ _ _ in Him may not die but have eternal life." (v16)

10 ☐ **Read Luke 19v10**

*Jesus (sometimes called The Son of Man) came to **rescue** us.*

"The Son of Man came to seek and to save the **l** _ _ _ ." (v10)

Extra Readings

11 ☐ **Read 1 John 4v10**

Why did God send Jesus?—because of His everlasting love for us.

"This is what **I** _ _ _ is: it is not that we have loved God, but that He loved us and sent His Son to be the means by which our sins are forgiven." (v10)

12 ☐ **Read Romans 4v25**

Jesus died for our sins—but He didn't stay dead! God brought Him back to life.

"Because of our sins He was handed over to die, and He was **r** _ _ _ _ _ to life in order to put us right with God." (v25)

Memory Verses about following Jesus

13 ☐ **Read John 15v12**

We are to love each other, just as Jesus loved us.

"My commandment is this: love one another, just as I love **y** _ _ ." (v12)

14 ☐ **Read John 15v14**

If we are Jesus' friends, we will want to obey Him.

"You are my **f** _ _ _ _ _ _ _ if you do what I command you." (v14)

15 ☐ **Read Galatians 5v22-23**

The Holy Spirit changes us to become more like Jesus.

"But the **S** _ _ _ _ _ produces love, joy, peace, patience, kindness, goodness, faithfulness, humility and self-control." (v22-23)

16 ☐ **Read Philippians 4v4**

Christians aren't always happy. But they have a deep down joy because Jesus is their Rescuer and King.

"Rejoice in the Lord always. I will say it again: **R** _ _ _ _ _ _ !" (v4)

17 ☐ **Read Hebrews 12v1-2**

Like an athlete, we must keep going, and never give up.

"Let us run with determination the **r** _ _ _ that lies before us." (v1)

18 ☐ **Read 1 Corinthians 10v13**

Sometimes we will be tempted to do wrong things. But God promises to give us a way out.

"God will not let you be tempted beyond what you can bear. But when you are tempted, He will also provide a **W** _ _ **O** _ _ so that you can stand up under it." (v13)

19 ☐ **Read Romans 8v15-16**

*If we are followers of Jesus, we can call God our **Father**.*

"The Spirit makes you God's children, and by Him we cry out to God, 'Abba, **F** _ _ _ _ _ .' " (v15)

20 ☐ **Read Romans 8v28**

God is always in control. His good purposes always work out.

"We know that in all things God works for **g** _ _ _ with those who love Him, those whom He has called according to His purpose." (v28)

Extra Readings

21 ☐ Read Ephesians 3v20-21
God is able to do far more than we can ever imagine!
"To Him who by means of His power working in us is **a** _ _ _ to do so much more than we can ever ask for, or even think of: to God be the glory in the church and in Christ Jesus for all time, for ever and ever! Amen." (v20-21)

Memory Verses about Prayer and the Bible

22 ☐ Read Matthew 6v9-13
Jesus taught His followers how to pray. (Often called The Lord's Prayer.)
"This, then, is how you should **p** _ _ _ : Our Father in heaven..." (v9)

23 ☐ Read 1 Thessalonians 5v16-18
We can pray to God anywhere, any time. There's loads to thank Him for, even when things seem hard.
"Be joyful always, pray at all times, be **t** _ _ _ _ _ _ _ in all circumstances." (v16-18)

24 ☐ Read Philippians 4v6-7
*We can pray about **everything**. We don't need to worry.*
"Don't **w** _ _ _ _ about anything, but in all your prayers ask God for what you need, always asking Him with a thankful heart." (v6)

25 ☐ Read 2 Timothy 3v16-17
The Bible is God's word to us. It shows us how to serve Him.
"All **S** _ _ _ _ _ _ _ _ _ is inspired by God." (v16)

26 ☐ Read Hebrews 4v12
*The Bible shows us when we're **not** following Jesus too. It helps us to change.*
"The word of God is alive and active, sharper than any double-edged **s** _ _ _ _ ." (v12)

WHAT NEXT?

We hope that **Table Talk** has helped you get into a regular habit of reading the Bible with your children.

There are twelve issues of **Table Talk** available. Each issue contains 65 full **Table Talk** outlines, plus 26 days of extra readings.

Available from your local Good Book Company website: **UK:** www.thegoodbook.co.uk
North America: www.thegoodbook.com
Australia: www.thegoodbook.com.au
New Zealand: www.thegoodbook.co.nz

THE NEXT ISSUE
Issue Five: The Promise Keeper

Issue Five of Table Talk explores the books of Mark, Numbers, Deuteronomy and Ephesians.

- Investigate who Jesus is and why He came in **Mark's** Gospel.
- Continue journeying with the Israelites in **Numbers** and **Deuteronomy**.
- Read one of Paul's prison letters—his letter to the **Ephesians**.